"In Rilke, we encounter a poet who holds together what often seems at odds: youth and wisdom; focus and freedom; devotion and doubt; God and the self. With Stephanie Dowrick and Mark S. Burrows we are in the safe hands of writers who are sensitive to this exquisite tension of Rilke's, and who also hold it themselves: their scholarship has the quality of music; their theological insights have the character of hospitality; their insights are appealing to the expert and the newcomer alike. With their combined knowledge of literature and culture, spirituality and poetry, their offering in *You Are the Future* is truly a wise way to live a life in the company of self and others." —**Pádraig Ó Tuama, PhD**, poet, theologian, and host of On Being's *Poetry Unbound*

"Two distinguished Rilke scholars bring their life-long pondering on and resonance with the poet's spiritual wisdom, a way of living shaped by awe, listening, and praise. Their probing of his 'wiser way' refuses to build a 'Rilke Museum,' inviting us rather to join the adventure of following his vision of 'living the questions' so that we, too, might become what he described as the 'bees of the invisible.' This volume explores the mysterious work of language with its unspoken depths, yielding a book that is as breathtaking and inspiring as Rilke himself is." —**Prof. Gotthard Fermor, PhD**, theologian, writer, and editor of Rainer Maria Rilke's *Das Stunden-Buch*

"This is a magnificent book, so generous, wise and loving. Anchored in the lived questions that Rilke celebrated, *You Are the Future* opens to fertile places for soul making and heart opening. Stephanie Dowrick and Mark Burrows each bring their lifetime of experience and scholarship to create a book for your lifetime of reading and reflection. Never could there be a timelier moment than now to take a deep dive into poetry of the soul, accompanied by writers of great heart, and with translations that sing of authenticity and inspiration. This is a book to savour, soaking up the rewards of stories, insights and provocations about the passage of our lives. It illuminates the ways of the world, and the capacity of poetry to hold us when all else falls away." —**Sally Gillespie, PhD**, author of *Climate Crisis and Consciousness: Re-imagining Our World and Ourselves*

"*You Are the Future* shows with piercing insight how Rilke's life and poetry offer a therapy of soul-making, a way of living soulfully in dark times—and what seem, at times, to be end times—by living into your deepest questions. What matters is to live a creative life, which is a key point in Jung's understanding of soul work, so that, as Rilke notes, "you can be a 'transformer of the earth,'" which is your "entire being, with all your soarings and stumblings," especially in those "dark hours" of your life and begin to sense that these moments or seasons invite you to embrace "a second life, timeless and wide." Dowrick and Burrows have written not just a book to peruse at one's leisure. They have written a text that invites, and even demands, a meditative attention. It is inspired and inspiring, insightful, and wise. Reading it I live the questions of my life, my work, and my relationships by sinking into the stillness of solitude and the serenity of silence. Then I began to hear the song that attunes my life to the breathing of all nature of which I am a part." —**Robert D. Romanyshyn, PhD**, author of *Leaning Toward the Poet: Eavesdropping on the Poetry of Everyday Life*

"From the first page of *You Are the Future*, I felt an aperture widening, both depth and dimension magnified, and was drawn into a more nuanced understanding of Rilke, yes, but also of some of the most perplexing questions about living a wiser way in these often soul-numbing times. All the way through to the very last page, I never lost a sense of amazement that poetries written a century ago held such profound and timeless wisdom for this incongruous moment in human history. In so many ways, this might be one book to never put down." —**Barbara Mahany**, author of *The Book of Nature* and *Slowing Time: Seeing the Sacred Outside Your Kitchen Door*

"Each of these short, wise teachings begin as nudges from Rilke, that poet-mystic who caused us to see God in our darkness, dreaming, and dawning. We live in the age of Rilke more than ever before. This is a book to remind us why we read." —**Jon M. Sweeney**, author of *Feed the Wolf* and *Nicholas Black Elk*

"*You Are the Future* guides us into Rilke's work through the details of his life and, in doing so, invites robust self-examination. Burrows' and Dowrick's writing mirrors Rilke's tender urgency, rejecting both the inattention and easy answers that consume our world." —**Benjamin Perry**, award-winning author of *Cry, Baby: Why Our Tears Matter*

YOU ARE THE FUTURE

LIVING THE QUESTIONS
with
RAINER MARIA RILKE

MARK S. BURROWS
&
STEPHANIE DOWRICK

Monkfish Book Publishing Company
Rhinebeck, New York

All translations of Rilke's poems and prose cited in this book are by Mark S. Burrows unless otherwise noted; those from *Prayers of a Young Poet* are used with the permission of Paraclete Press and those from the *Sonnets to Orpheus* with the permission of Monkfish Book Publishing Company.

Paperback ISBN 978-1-958972-53-3
eBook ISBN 978-1-958972-54-0

Library of Congress Cataloging-in-Publication Data

Names: Burrows, Mark S., 1955- author. | Dowrick, Stephanie, author.
Title: You are the future : living the questions with Rainer Maria Rilke /
   Mark S. Burrows & Stephanie Dowrick.
Description: Rhinebeck, New York : Monkfish Book Publishing Company, 2024.
Identifiers: LCCN 2024017156 (print) | LCCN 2024017157 (ebook) | ISBN
   9781958972533 (paperback) | ISBN 9781958972540 (ebook)
Subjects: LCSH: Rilke, Rainer Maria, 1875-1926--Criticism and
   interpretation. | LCGFT: Literary criticism.
Classification: LCC PT2635.I65 Z646 2024 (print) | LCC PT2635.I65 (ebook)
   | DDC 831/.912--dc23/eng/20240522
LC record available at https://lccn.loc.gov/2024017156
LC ebook record available at https://lccn.loc.gov/2024017157

Book and cover design by Colin Rolfe

Monkfish Book Publishing Company
22 East Market Street, Suite 304
Rhinebeck, New York 12572
(845) 876-4861
monkfishpublishing.com

For Mark's granddaughter, Leela Sophia,
and Stephanie's grandchildren: Madeleine Grace, Charles Garry,
& Lux Lowanna.

You are our future.

CONTENTS

"Nothing is more beautiful than beginnings.
Each becoming is as sacred as at the start."

Rainer Maria Rilke (1875–1926)

A NOTE TO READERS

There is only one way: Go into yourself…
Be attentive to what rises up within you.

—Rainer Maria Rilke, *Letters to a Young Poet*

Somewhat unusually, this book can be read sequentially—but need not
be. Each essay-style chapter is intended to open you to a rich circling
of a particular theme by engaging the poem or short prose extract that
illuminates it. This approach also suggests that you might well begin
with the "question" that engages you with the greatest immediacy, find-
ing your way through others as you move through the book at a pace
entirely of your own choosing.

Some details about Rainer Maria Rilke's writings and life have
therefore been deliberately repeated. This means that each chapter, no
matter where you start, offers sufficient context to respond to whatever
the poem, or our conversations with it, raises for you. After all, your
own way of "living the questions" is always the adventure we wish to
encourage.

Another slight oddity: sometimes the deepening question addresses
you as "you"; sometimes it takes you directly into a first-person inquiry
or raises a concern that we widely share in this complex time. While this
wasn't our conscious intention, we are honoring it because that uneven,
undulating terrain best prompts fresh thinking—and welcomes the sur-
prises that might startle us into new seeing and encourage us on the way.
Without our consciously intending it, that also reflects Rilke's own play

with the intimate "you" in his poems, bringing us closer to him, to the universality of our best intentions, and to *you*.

Mark S. Burrows and Stephanie Dowrick
Camden, Maine (USA) & Sydney, Australia

ON CHOOSING A WISER WAY

"Being here matters so much."

—from the *Ninth Elegy*

Among the many astonishing gifts of human consciousness, language surely stands supreme. It is with and through language that we create meaning inwardly and connect with one another. Because language is so familiar, it is easy to take its near-miraculous potentials for granted. That is, until a masterful use of language sufficiently startles us to re-think what language can do. How much it adds to *being*. That's what true poets can give, in a form condensed and nuanced enough to change something more than our thinking: to change our "view."

Take these single lines, selected virtually at random:

> *Birds fly silently through us…*
> *Who, if I cried out, would hear me among the ranks of angels?*
> *The work of seeing is done; / now take up the heart-work…*
> *Earth, isn't it this that you long for: to rise invisibly within us?*
> *This is the wondrous play of powers / moving through things to*
> *   serve them.*
> *But the darkness holds everything within itself…*

Many of these lines return in the chapters that follow. All of them—and so many, many more—come from the poet Rainer Maria Rilke, who was born in Prague in 1875 and died at the young age of fifty-one in the Swiss village of Montreux in 1926. As such lines suggest, he was a writer described by his lifelong confidante Lou Andreas-Salomé as one who "learned to prove himself through the simplest workaday things and a reverent approach to even the poor and unblessed hours of this existence."

Rilke's survival as a poet who transcends both time and place is already rare. Even remarkable. So are his gifts of imagery and insight. Those insights, found through language, arise from Rilke's own never-straightforward life, his startling unorthodoxy of view, and his commitment to an openness of mind and perspective that nurtured his instincts.

He himself saw language as a tool of inquiry, sent out like a "probe" to the limits of human imagination and experience as "bees of the invisible," as he once famously put it. This adds up to a quite new way not just of seeing life, but of more fully embracing and valuing it. *All of it.* This allows for a very special kind of wisdom: hard-won, expansive, transcendent. It is a wisdom that Rilke makes available to us through his poetry, primarily, but also through the treasure trove of his letters. For it is there that he poured out his innermost feelings, speaking as much to himself as to the letter's recipient—and to us, his later readers. Why? Because, to repeat Rilke's insistent claim, *being here matters so much.*

For all that, we don't see this as a book just *about* the wisdom found so amply in Rilke's writing. We see this book—and have experienced this in our writing of it—as a guide *into* wisdom: a new kind of wisdom that lifts burdens, adds vibrant texture, allows for greater sensuality and for an unrushed contemplation of what brings joy as well as raises questions. The kind that leads you to value your own experiences, as well as those of others.

We write here in conversation with Rilke and each other, opening to a "wiser way" than is more generally offered in our hectic, demanding societies, where individuality is so highly praised and our inevitable interconnectedness is so poorly understood. It is a wisdom, we trust, that is accessible, even contagious. It might well enable you to ground your life in what the ancients knew as the "transcendentals": "the true, the good, and the beautiful." Those are collective attributes we find singly and learn to live socially.

We can put it even more simply. Our approach in this book locates these life-shaping realities not *outside* ourselves but rather *within* our own experiences. Within *your* experiences. For what matters in finding such a "way" is the discovery that *we* are the bearers of truth; that *we* are actors capable of goodness in our lives; that *we* are those who have the capacity to reveal beauty—or, as Rilke once put it, to "offer your beauty always / without calculation and talk."

Through this re-shaping of wisdom, and a new or renewed valuing of your unique inwardness, you may find that you are not simply one who lives between your past and your future. Rilke's writing offers something more provocative and alluring than that. He suggests in one of his early poems that "you *are* the future." You! As he himself wrote that line: *Du bist die Zukunft.*

Who is that "you"? He leaves the reference tantalizingly unspecified.

Is it the "you" of the divine one he often addressed simply as "Lord" but could equally call "neighbor" or "friend"? Is it the "you" of the poet himself? Or the "you" of the reader? Rilke refused, characteristically, to define whom he is addressing. For in the deepest things of life, the truest things of the heart, the most enduring things of the soul, *these three are not different.* Not distinct. Not separable.

You are the future.

The poet's claim invites us, as we explore throughout this book, to see ourselves as those who are *ripening*; whose lives are not set in stone but are *unfolding*; whose present is always one of *becoming,* three active, evocative words he often relied upon in his poems. Of course, the claim might be one we do best to *receive* as a question, one that invites us to live our way into as we ourselves ripen and unfold within the wealth of allusions the "you" carries. Because, in truth, your deepest identity is not definable, even by language. It belongs to the flow that courses through everything—from the smallest subatomic measures within each cell to the immensities of an expanding universe. You, at every moment in your life, are not simply part of that flow. *You* are the flow. And yes: you are *the future.*

The vibrancy of Rilke's wisdom, as we have come to understand it—and as it has helped us better understand *ourselves*—invites us *to read our own lives,* and to do so with curiosity, respect, and even excitement. We find ourselves opening to the spacious and generous *Yes* that courses through his writings, an affirmation he consistently voiced without a hint of sentimentality or avoidance of life's complexity and sorrows.

As a guide, Rilke is not infallible. We welcome that. But even when his own confusions overwhelm him, something in the momentum of his work rings with an almost irresistible allure. He often stumbled. Yet again and again we find him—as he put it in one of his early poems—desiring nothing less than "the dark held in each unending demise / and the light-trembling game in every rise."

*

With increasing intensity through our many conversations as this book took shape, we found ourselves provoked and inspired, moved, too, by the witness of Rilke's writings. Against the flimsy ambitions of what he critically saw as the "managed" culture of modernity, this exceptional poet sought a way of being that recognized "a part of our existence" found shape in what he called "invisibility," a spiritual reality that could not be seen or organized, nor reduced to dogma, nor controlled. This book, our work, is a very personal response to Rilke's now-famous call to *live the questions* without striving for superficial, untested, or outworn answers.

Such living takes courage. It also takes a willed, chosen trust in what Rilke called your "inner-ness": a sense that "answers" do not always come best from outside yourself, and that "answers" do not always come quickly when the questions or challenges matter.

In a world facing crises on many fronts, it is understandable that that we may long for quick relief to stem the tide of personal confusion and anxious self-doubt. We may also long for greater clarity around the central existential questions about what life is *for*. Rarely, though, will this lead to a deeper, more stabilizing trust in facing life *as it is*. Which is to say, life with all its burdens and blessings, contradictions and consolations, problems—and possibilities.

Living into the questions takes you inward while also expanding your outer view: "forwarding" you, rather than holding you back. Living into your own deepest questions—rather than rushing toward familiar solutions or placating answers—is a choice. It is a choice that no one can make for you. Rilke instinctively understood all this.

*

"Nothing is more beautiful than beginnings. Each becoming is as sacred as at the start." With these bold words, Rilke declared a conviction that we shared in creating *You Are the Future*. As two writers who live on different continents, and whose personal and professional lives have followed notably dissimilar trajectories, we bring to this work unusually varied experiences and perspectives. That seems near-perfect for meeting readers who will look to Rilke—and to us—for thinking that is authentically liberating; that is invitational and alluring; that encourages curiosity as well as renewed self-trust. And that draws on poetry—of all things—to open the way into greater possibility of heart and mind.

Rilke brought the two of us together. We met through our published work on Rilke's writings, both as the sublime poet he is and as a truly original thinker about life and our engagement with it. As a poet, Rilke knew that our primary task in this life was to indwell life with spaciousness and generosity. That's an odd concept perhaps, but it becomes meaningful everywhere in his poetry, letters, and commentaries on life.

He himself was undeniably a complicated and at times bewildering person. The many reasons why we were and remain so attracted to him, however, include his persistent calls to discover *the wholeness that we carry within ourselves*. In a time when trust itself can seem to be fragmenting, this seeking and guiding into wholeness is immense, backed by his call, as he put it, to "let everything happen to you: beauty and terror."

We trust his radical embrace of the contradictions that many shy away from. Plus—supremely—we have, in our writing here, wholeheartedly responded to his magnificent challenge that we could and can live into our deepest questions with honesty and accelerating meaning, even when we are enduring a bleakness that Rilke also understood. Reading Rilke soon lets you read your own life more thoughtfully, more sensually, more compassionately—which, after all, is the most vital reading of all. His poems may function like mirrors, offering a capacity to see yourself whole ("…let everything happen…"), and not for what you do or have—or fail at, or lack.

Our chapters reflect this. They can be read singly, guided by a theme that probes some essential dimension of our lives. Often enough, the questions we explore—and you, with us—touch upon the uncertainties we might more usually have seen as *problems to be overcome*. Rilke, by contrast, views them as places of spaciousness where you might learn to begin anew or open to a more generous perspective, or a more thoughtful one that eases the tension that comes when we even half believe there is only one way, or one "perfect" answer in our still-unfolding, singularly complex lives. They remind us that, beyond the urgencies required simply to survive, the source and gift of life beckons us to thrive.

*

We have shaped *You Are the Future* around Rilke's poems and excerpts from his writings, approaching them as windows through which we might see with greater fidelity what is possible—for us and others. As each chapter circles a single poem, it offers a self-knowing that both relates to the chosen topic and extends beyond it. You may be drawn by instinct to one theme before others. Choose freely. You may take one poem "to heart" and find yourself indifferent to another.

We chose the poems instinctively, then explored that instinctive choice through the sieve of our own separate needs and seeking, consciously living into them, consciously avoiding the safer "high ground" of abstractions. In his *Letters to a Young Poet*, Rilke wrote:

Let your judgments follow their quiet, undisturbed evolution, which, like all progress, must come from deep within and cannot be pressured or hurried in any way. It's all about carrying to term and giving birth. To let every impression and every seed of a feeling realize itself on its own, in the dark, in the unconveyable, the unconscious, beyond the reach of your understanding, and to await with deep humility and patience the hour when a new clarity is born; this alone is to live artistically, in understanding as in creation.

The poem that follows was written when Rilke was still a young man. It comes in the opening section of *The Book of Hours*, prayer/poems he wrote in the persona of an elderly Orthodox monk, though the poet himself was anything but that. Singly and as a whole, those poems are unpredictable in their view of the divine. They do not reflect teachings from the institutional church of his day, which Rilke viewed as dogmatically insistent and patriarchal. He was also allergic to a piety like his own mother's which was narrow and sentimental. Rilke rebelled from all this, once suggesting that "…we all come away from the deathbed of [our] childhood god dressed in mourning, but as [we] walk with increasing confidence and festiveness, God's resurrection takes place *within* [us]."

For precisely this reason he could invoke such tenderness when writing about "God" and our yearning to be inwardly "touched" and perhaps "remembered."

> God speaks to each of us before making us,
> then wanders with us silently out of the night.
> But words uttered before that beginning,
> clouded words only, are these:
>
> "Go, you who are sent out by your senses,
> go to the edge of your longing.
> Give me form with your life.

Grow like a fire behind things
so that their shadows, spreading all about,
cover me always and utterly.
Let everything happen to you: beauty and terror.
Only go on; no feeling outreaches you.
Don't let yourself part with me.
Nearby is the land
you call life.

You'll know it
by its earnestness.
Give me your hand."

Give me your hand. Rilke's God is not in a separate realm. Rilke's God is here, now, sometimes forgotten but never forgetting. His "God" has nothing to do with established orthodoxies, religious or otherwise, and everything to do with an authentic embrace of life in which inner and outer, immanence and transcendence, are finally seen as one—and as expressions of "the Whole," as he often put it. That Rilke himself is frequently referred to as a "spiritual poet" in the sense that he sought to find and express meaning (and largely found it in art—and life) is surely true. But his explorations of the great existential themes stood out for their unconventionality in his time, and perhaps even more so in ours when so often "belief" has slid into a rigid and narrow dogmatism that becomes difficult or impossible to challenge.

Throughout *The Book of Hours*, in which Rilke addresses "God" as "you," he describes this "you" with a startling array of metaphors: as an "ancient tower," as something "dark and like a clump of a hundred roots," the "dawning one," the "darkness from which [we] come," "dreamer," and so on. The effect of this is to see the Divine present in the unexpected and certainly most intimate dimensions of life. That resonates strongly with us. In these poems God is "neighbor," "the soft evening hour," and the "rhyme [that] still rustles in [our] ear." "God" is also "the mysterious one around whom time stood hesitantly still."

Crucially, this "you" whom Rilke so familiarly addresses can be found in *every* moment of life: in awe and bliss, in agony and despair. Years of reading and re-reading these poems cannot diminish their power to disrupt familiar assumptions. Or to provoke as well as delight readers. There's so much raw sensuality here, so much "real world" physicality and earthiness along with unrivaled metaphors. This certainly inspires. It "languages" what might otherwise remain unthought. What's specific about Rilke, though, is that his is an inspiration that depends on art, and for that reason also on *your receptivity*, coming out of a refusal to shy from the shadows or retreat into hardened certainties.

As Rilke expressed it in a letter, referring to the French painter, Paul Cézanne: "Surely all art is the result of one's having been in danger, of having gone through and experienced things all the way to the end, where no one can go any further. Therein lies the enormous aid the work of art brings to the life of the one who must make it." Yes, we are "transported," not "away from" but further into life.

*

In a way that may be tricky for contemporary readers to grasp, Rilke loathed the idea of his work being merely "helpful." He also had little time for formal literary criticism which he regarded as arid and unfeeling. In these chapters, we invite you into the subtle depths of his poems where they meet your own instincts and senses and challenge your intellect. The contradictions present in his work add texture. So, too, do the vulnerabilities they allow for and the tenderness they evoke. Again, in *The Book of Hours*, the poet who would later shudder at the thought of conventional "religion" was writing:

> I love You, You softest of laws
> by which we ripened in our wrestling;
> You great homesickness that we'd not mastered.
>
> [...] Let Your hand rest on the ledge of heaven

And mutely endure what we darkly do to You.

*

In countless ways, writing and reading have become our most nuanced and potentially profound uses of language. It is a relative inner steadiness—born from self-trust—that reading brings, while also allowing for moments of inner wildness, untamedness, spontaneity, plus a living *into* life rather than viewing it as a spectator. As a young man, Rilke wrote:

> Self-transformation is precisely what life is, and human relationships, as an extract of life, are the most change-able of all, rising and falling from minute to minute, and lovers are those in whose relationship and contact not a single moment resembles any other.... There are such relationships which must be a very great, almost unbear-able happiness, but these can happen only between very rich natures and those who are abundantly ordered and composed; they can unite only two wide, deep, indi-vidual worlds.... For one person to love another: that is perhaps the most difficult of all our tasks, the ultimate, the final test and proof, the work for which all other effort is but preparation.

It is undeniable that what should be instinctive, natural, and reward-ing is now frequently fraught or utterly dismaying. This is not true of romantic love only. It is also true of our love for humankind, for the planet, for justice, truth, beauty, and decency.

*

As we prepared to write this book, we found ourselves increasingly excited about what it would mean to approach these questions collabo-ratively, while welcoming our differences in how we "read" Rilke. We are interpreting not poetry only but even more so our lives within the very separate contexts in which we live: Mark as an American who has spent a good part of his life, and most of the last decade, living and working in Germany; Stephanie as a third-generation New Zealander who spent sixteen years in the UK and Germany before moving to Australia in the 1980s. Collaboration never added up to sameness for us. No two chapters in our book are uniform or, we hope, predictable. While our convictions have much in common, we are not always of one mind—any more than you need to be with us.

Our intention has never been to give you "our" Rilke. He is not ours to give. We have complementary gifts: Mark's as a poet, translator, and teacher devoted to exploring the mysterious energies of the spiritual life, and as a scholar of the literature of Western mysticism; Stephanie's through years of working in book publishing, many more years of writing both fiction and non-fiction, and through the practice of psychotherapy and ministry. Ours is an appreciation of each other—in the presence of Rilke—that has deepened and ripened here.

Where we are united is in our wholehearted endorsing of the variety of ways in which our human family seeks meaning. We also welcome paradox, echoing Rilke in another of his poems from *The Book of Hours*:

> Whoever reconciles the many paradoxes of life
> and grasps them in a symbol gratefully
> are those who drive
> the noisy crowd from the palace
> and celebrate differently....

Finding images as well as ideas that jolt, challenge, or enchant may allow you—as it has us—to view life-questions with fresh curiosity. Or patience. Or a fierce determination to embrace all of who you are, and not only part.

*

The priorities of Western society take us away from real health, not toward it. Rilke understood such states of mind and lived them, sometimes more and other times less gracefully. As a modernist, he feared the accelerating commodification of human life—the turn from ritual and story, the loss of awe and wonder, the alienation from the natural world, the push to see one another as "economic units." This has worsened in the century since his death. Yet Rilke sustains hope: "To be here is immense," he wrote. He trusted, too, that each of us holds within ourselves—in concert with others—the wisdom we need and long to find, not simply to survive but also to value life consciously. As he once put it,

> The best thing in life is that we each hold everything within ourselves: our fate, our future, even the entire breadth of our life and world. Of course, there are moments when we find it difficult to be with ourselves and to endure our own company. Yet it also happens that *there are times when we hold ourselves more authentically than ever before and bind ourselves to something outside of us as important incidents shift our center to what we find strange and bring us into contact with others* [our italics].

*

If the poet is not on every page here, then he is *behind* every page and *between* the words that found their way to this book. We have sought and found resonances for our times: a prescience about life, the universe, our place in it that surely exceeds any conscious intention on Rilke's part. For all the many years each of us has worked on/with/around Rilke, we were to the end of this writing open to startlement; and received it. Ours is a friendship sustained by a conscious commitment to language as well as to the seeking that goes beyond language, while consciously appreciating that neither of us has come into and through adult life tied to a single language or culture, nor to any "set of instructions" defined by others. We share that, in different ways, with Rilke.

We know, too, that both as a poet and as a person, Rilke is many things to many people. We respect that. He's now widely translated for English-language readers, a considerable feat given the lyric voice in which he wrote. Sometimes these renderings come in translations that express more about his interpreters than about Rilke. But spaciousness is key here, key to living into greater spaciousness—or what the poet came to refer to as "the Open." And, yes: key to your receptivity.

Across the arc of our collaboration, we have shared the conviction Rilke expressed in an early journal entry when he insisted that "the artist's way must be this: to bridge obstacle after obstacle and to build step after step, until at last [she] can gaze into [her]self; not straining, not forced, not on [her] tiptoes, but calmly and clearly as into a landscape." This has allowed us a writing ease, even in the moments of confusion that seem mysteriously to precede the biggest hurrahs.

We have been and remain grateful for this chance to write together, to deepen a true friendship through the arduous, exhilarating processes necessary to be worthy of our subject matter. It was in the writing that we came to see this process as a "wiser way," one that points to a more embracing future. It is in the living, that we—with you—celebrate this.

CHAPTER 1

TO BE A BEGINNER

The hour bows down and stirs me
with a clear and ringing stroke;
my senses tremble. I feel that I can—
and seize the forming day.

Nothing was yet done before I beheld it,
and every becoming stood still;
my ways of seeing are ripe, and, like a bride,
to each one comes the thing each wills.

Nothing is too small for me, and I love it anyway
and paint it on the golden base and large—
and hold it high; and I don't know *whose*
soul this might yet free.

—from "The Book of Monastic Life,"
The Book of Hours

"Ah, how good it is to be among people who are reading," wrote the then-emerging poet, Rainer Maria Rilke. And don't you know this feeling, too? Perhaps for Rilke, perhaps for you, reading is an experience of both intimacy and solitude unlike almost any other. Between bright covers, disguising the years of change, growth, rewriting, you can dive deep. And surface only when you are ready.

As the words from a page meet you, as *you* meet the words on a page, a connection happens. Or it can. Our ideas, stories, and experiences invariably mix with and sometimes challenge the ideas you already have. And perhaps not your ideas only, but your assumptions, beliefs, and preconceptions as well. No reader is a blank slate! On the contrary, a lifetime of conversations, reflections, reading, forgetting, remembering, feeling excited or feeling flat makes for a richly fertile "innerscape." Yet, readers trust, with room for more as their own thoughts meet the thoughts of the writer.

Rilke captured this with typical physicality, for we don't read only with our eyes. Reading is a *bodily* experience. So is writing, and Rilke accurately said of readers that they do "... not always remain bent over the pages...." In his experience, readers "often lean back and close their eyes over a line they have been reading again, and its meaning spreads through their blood." That has surely been our experience with his work, and we trust it will be for you as well.

We are generally relatively still as we read. Yet reading—and reflecting—is anything but passive. An active shift may take place in the experience, shifting how it is that you see the world or yourself in the world. You are adding others' experiences, including Rilke's, to your own. Your reading deepens your place in and understanding of our wondrously diverse human family. And we "...*don't know* whose/*soul this might yet free*." Nor do we always know what seed within ourselves is now watered. Or when a needed freshness begins.

> The hour bows down and stirs me
> with a clear and ringing stroke;
> my senses tremble. I feel that I can—
> and seize the forming day.

What might it be like to respond more fully to a "clear and ringing stroke" and open yourself to "seize [this] forming day"? To follow the thrum of intuition rather than your more conditioned mind and often hesitant intellect? To give yourself permission to revive a hope, to see a complex situation more simply, to dive deeper and find a reservoir of trust within?

Not to "linger indefinitely at daybreak"—as a different poem of Rilke's warns against—but to move into the heart of the day with courage and authenticity?

So much in our world dampens our passion. Shrinks our horizons. Tells us what we must fear. What we can't do. So much in our world urges caution, compliance with others' norms; with pessimism and pettiness. Is that the "forming day" you most wish to seize? Perhaps not.

Take your time with this. Take *your* time with this. Time is what we sell, barter, give away, and where frequently we believe we have little or no control. "*I have no time to…be fully alive*," is the subtext of much of our suffering. "*We have no time for each other…*" is the subtext to many of our intimate relationship failures. "*I have no time to know myself*," underpins an essential aloneness that crowds of contacts cannot assuage.

What would free up within you if you dared imagine every day—and *today*—as a new beginning? Not for a moment either discarding or discounting the accumulated wisdom of your existence so far, but as an opportunity to experience life, *your* life, with greater insight, consideration, or inspiration? With greater curiosity, risk, boldness—or gentleness—not in someone else's way, but in your own?

What might it be like if, as Rilke once put it, you could risk trusting that the "dark hours" of your life might bring a sense not of insufficiency or despair but of your continuously unfolding awakening? Of possibility? Of your *becoming*? Or, as he put it in a letter written in the aftermath of the shattering First World War, "If [your] angel condescends to come, it will be because you have persuaded him, not with your tears but by your humble decision to start afresh: to be a beginner (*ein Anfänger zu sein*)!"

*

To live into our full humanity, we need to accept that life necessarily challenges as well as supports us. We may have to abandon some of our childish ideas about fairness. Or what should happen but does not. Much "unfairness" is structural, calculated and inhumane. Yet it may be empowering to see also that the individual questions that affect us arise within a social context that *we ourselves are affecting* as well. By "per-suading [our angel] to come with a humble decision to start afresh…?" Maybe.

There is an infinite wealth we could learn directly from the earth and its rhythms of renewal, while also learning to protect it better—and, with it, ourselves. An appreciation of others' lives is central here, as is an appreciation of the wondrous physical world so gravely threatened by plunder, stupidity, and selfishness. Rilke wrote, joyfully, "It is spring again. The earth is like a child that knows poems by heart." Such appre-ciation must begin and continue with cherishing the gift of your own life. No life is free of anguish. Wisdom, like patience, is learned in the moment, and often enough on the run.

We are part of a whole. This comes through everywhere in the poems we have chosen. Simultaneously, we are awesomely unique. This awareness has flourished within us separately as we have worked on this book. It has brought each of us strength, most especially in times of ill-ness or intense concern for beloved others. For us, for you, it also allows for genuine compassion as we include in our self-acceptance what we might otherwise ban to the shadows. *Nothing is too small for me, and I love it anyway…*

After all, your well of inner resources is irreplaceable. It's discov-ered through myriad experiences, including the harshest. But let's not romanticize forced "beginnings." Not all of us will survive them. Every hour, every second, individual lives are cut short, turned upside down, with immeasurable effect also on those closest to them. How do you "begin again" from that place? Slowly, we would say. Small step by very small step. And only with the discovery of self-compassion plus a con-scious acceptance that for the rest of your life your sense of self—and your understanding of life's fragility and arbitrariness—will be forever changed.

Changed for the better? We can hope so. But that is not something to demand or expect from other people. Or yourself. None of us knows what hard "beginnings" have already occurred in another person's life. Judgment is especially unwarranted here. We need to think long and hard about any conscious or unconscious demand for a bouncy new beginning when someone has lost the person who is their "rock." Or when they are dispossessed by war, poverty, bigotry, or violence. Or when mental or physical illness robs them of a trusted sense of self.

We know first-hand what a small step of beginning can cost when despair beckons. Yet it is a willed choosing of life over death: *as sacred as that*. In many such instances, to get out of bed and get through another day is beginning enough. (If this is you as you read these words, our hearts are with you.) From wherever you are, and whoever you are, Rilke's words return like a recitative, a mantra, an arising: *You are the future*. You. We. All.

*

How stabilizing it is, then, to discover that our very "ways of seeing" can be "ripe"—or can ripen:

> …my ways of seeing are ripe, and, like a bride,
> to each one comes the thing each wills.

It is at least some degree of "ripeness"—or readiness—that lets you live more firmly within this world, within your body, within the particularities and universalities of *your* life—even when your outer circumstances would seem to reduce you.

"Ripe" is a word as sensual as any other. Our deepest questions cannot be effectively considered simply as abstractions. Ideas and ideals come to life only through your living them: "good" experiences and "not so good" equally. In fact, our major theme in this book—living your questions with spaciousness and depth, with courage and trust—has very much become a testimony to those difficult hours when you have no choice but to pause and to seek a new response, a new way, or just greater gentleness, self-trust as well as patience. *To begin again*: the choice itself bestows a blessing.

Almost uniquely, and surely as a product of his own physical and emotional suffering as well as a craving for life's fullness, Rilke knew that difficulties, far from being problems to be avoided, are ways into our own creativity. They could be the exact catalyst that's inviting you to "leave the familar room where you know everything"—as Rilke wrote in another poem (see Ch. 9). "Knowing everything" shuts portals. "Living your questions" opens them.

Such self-honoring may become a chance to discover the fertile wisdom already waiting in your own life, plus how to live into its depths. Not "someday..." or "when..." or "after I have...". But in the very presence of your fears, hesitations, and unresolved questions. "Nothing is too small for me, and I love it anyway..." A life lived with greater authenticity is a life lived in "heartfulness." We spare others so much suffering, as well as ourselves, when we can take for granted that we will make mistakes, misjudge situations, fall or fail repeatedly—but can nonetheless rise up again into the future unfolding in this moment, now. *You are the future.*

No rich inner life or meaningful care for others is forged from successes only. Or from "everything fitting with my agenda." Success may be highly desirable. Our societies certainly say so. Yet isn't it your own intuitions, inner promptings—and a wisdom born from the wholeness of your experiences—that will call you forward, if you can allow that? This then becomes a beckoning, a summoning that invites you to live what Rilke calls "a second life, timeless and wide." This is a life of *your* choosing, *your* values, *your* vision of what freedom and fullness might mean.

*

Would this excitement, or perhaps flickering trust, give you the *fortitude* (such a lovely old-fashioned word) to act on your most generous desires? To begin again through a fresh trusting of your inner resources, ripening a new way of seeing? Would it give you the confidence to accept others and their inevitable complexities a little more easily? To widen your heart to accept both the serene and the stormy seasons of your life with courage? To dare to "live the questions" of your life rather than trying too quickly or anxiously to answer them? To open yourself to a quiet "innerness" that may lead you through the difficulties you face? To discover that *you are the future?*

This adds up to what Rilke so marvelously named as "heart-work" (*Herz-Werk*), bringing to greater awareness *all* that you carry deep within you. This takes healing into wholeness, something we both reflect upon in these pages and in life (leaving out no part of ourselves as best we can).

It is no accident that poetry, of all literary forms, can best circumvent the so-called "rational," linear, often limiting ways of seeing in which we are so thoroughly trained. Poetry—true poetry—sidesteps much of that conditioning. It teases, challenges, tightens our vision, and all at once frees it. Poetry works in images and paradoxes. It expands the horizons of language. It provokes as often as it soothes, puzzles as well as entices. Poetry is often highly visual, engaging all the senses. It plays with memory and surpasses it. It reveals truths, the deep sort that resist explanation, moving past the realm of mere facts.

As the late Irish poet, John O'Donohue, gorgeously put it:

> There is a relentless search [in our society] for the factual and this quest often lacks warmth or reverence. At a certain stage in our lives we may wake up to the urgency of life, how short it is. Then the quest for truth becomes the ultimate project.... If we choose to journey on the path of truth, it then becomes a sacred duty to walk hand in hand with beauty.

We took up Rilke's invitation to "heart-work" with every stage of our writing of this book. We learned to trust it, even knowing such "work" is sometimes elusive and found only by enduring. But *you*, what if you were to sense your way into your own wisdom with a little more confidence, knowing that this "wisdom" of yours, of ours, of Rilke's, is both your very own and inevitably shared? That it looks forward from each beginning, while never losing sight of the value of what has gone before?

"I live my life in widening circles," wrote Rilke in another poem from the *Book of Hours* that we explore in a later chapter. What we are evoking here is a kind of mindfulness, letting us be present to *what is*, and simultaneously open to *what is emerging*—both within us and all around us: the beginnings that each new moment can bring, again and again, when we view this potent present unbound from the past and open to our being and becoming. *You are the future.*

*

Not everyone has an urge "to live artistically," Rilke suggested in his celebrated collection of *Letters to a Young Poet*. Perhaps you've read them, a slender collection of ten letters written to a younger poet by the only slightly older Rilke, opening the young poet, Franz Kappus, to a wisdom he had not yet found in himself? These letters have become Rilke's best-known prose writing and remain astonishingly relevant to those of us seeking to live with greater appreciation and meaning.

What Rilke meant here by "artistically" points toward a freshness of looking, which is what beginnings demand and give. And, even more, a call to live *authentically*, to live passionately, from life's depths. From *your* depths. In our stridently materialistic world, this invitation might seem confusing. Even scary. What does it have to do with "doing well"? Making a success of "things" when appearances seem to matter most?

I'm not an artist, you might be saying to yourself. *I am no poet. I don't know if I even like poetry. That's not for me.* But Rilke was after something entirely different from whatever you do on the "outside." He was pointing to what you make of your *inner* life. To "live artistically" means seeing how life is always inviting you "to let every impression and every seed of a feeling reach completion in its own way—in the dark, in the unsayable and unconscious, in experiences unreachable by reason alone—and, with deep humility and patience, to await the hour when a new clarity might come forth."

*

Here, and in the chapters that follow, is our way of discovering, with you, what it might mean "to let every impression and every seed of a feeling reach completion *in its own way.*" Which no one can do for you; which you must *choose* to seek in and within your own life.

Beginnings are everywhere in these pages as they are in life, shifting—often subtly and without demand—how we might regard ourselves. How we might go beyond what we have been taught to be. How we might resist the temptations of bitterness. Or resentment. Or any degree of inner harshness. And move forward to make the future. How we might live alongside others, and in the complexity and beauty and challenge of our awesome shared physical world, with greater ease and appreciation. It is the appreciation of this physical world—an awareness of its fragility and ours—that will turn our urgent environmental efforts into willing acts of love.

This search for more vitalizing beginnings speaks to a recognition of your choices, and to that necessary pause reminding you of choice: that you are not a victim of unconscious drives or impetuous impulses. This increased level of consciousness is vital to discovering your own capacity for agency and freedom. *No one can do this search for you.*

And yet we are, every one of us, part of a greater whole. This was a steadiness of view and experiencing that Rilke relied upon; it is also ours. We belong to that "whole" and, in that belonging, to each other. Even a faint glimpse of the truth of our interdependence is to be welcomed. The companionship of this book is directly reflected in its creation. It grew from years of friendship and deep mutual respect between the two of us as writers, drawing from the wellspring of Rilke's writings. We know that this is not a book either of us could have written alone. Nor without the significant diversity of our lived experiences. Nor without an embracing of that central paradox and truth: we are one; we are many; and only together do we belong to "the Whole." Empathy, along with empathic imagination, is our lodestone, yet understood as much in its absence as in its lifesaving, life-giving presence.

Stephanie's life work has included years as a book publisher, largely in the UK and also Australia, and many more years as an Australian-based writer of both fiction and a wide range of exploratory books somewhat like this one, plus training and work as a psychotherapist and as an interfaith minister and retreat leader. Through all that, her lifelong passion for peace-keeping and social justice has sustained her spiritually and professionally, as has her intense commitment to her children and their children, in part coming out of a premature and shaky independence following a childhood when her own mother died far too young. She has lived in six countries, her earlier adult years echoing the unsettled pattern of Rilke's own life. Across the span of her life, Stephanie has discovered—with Rilke—that opening into an embracing spiritual perspective that is both intimate and universal is not easily achieved yet privileged in the seeking. Poetry is one portal; reflecting on and within the necessary messiness, contradictions, and ambivalence of everyday life—with its myriad joys as well as challenges—is another.

Mark's life as a writer, teacher, and bilingual translator has been inspired by the sense of being part of "the Whole," a conviction central in Rilke's later writings. It is that awareness of how nature and culture—the inner life and the outer world—belong together, and when we ignore or renounce that coherence, as is often the case in late modernity, our work is to bring a renewed attentiveness and vulnerability to the work of healing. It was Rilke, in those *Letters*, who invited us to "believe in a love that is being stored up for you like a legacy, and trust that there is in this love a strength and a blessing so large that you can travel as far as you wish without having to step outside it." Through the vision of poetry, most particularly, he has discovered what it means to open oneself to the risks and discoveries of that journey, an adventure shaped by living into "the Whole" and a consequential commitment to personal and societal transformation. Toward that end, the writing of poetry and the work of translation have shaped his calling, inspired by the creative energies of "unfolding" and "ripening"—those familiar words in Rilke's lexicon—that constitute the unique alchemy of that lifework.

*

When Rilke speaks of living "artistically" he offers you—as he has offered us—an invitation to live an *engaged* life, a life that takes promptings from the inside, from your heart, mind, and soul, and not just from what your portion of "the world" thinks. This takes determination as well as commitment. Living by conventions set by others is safe and often alluring. We *want* to belong. We want to fit in. Conformity has obvious rewards. It may also be confining, though, particularly when *Who am I?* extends beyond the most obvious labels you have for yourself—or others have for you. What it takes to break out of such bondage is a conviction that you are a whole self, a becoming self, worthy of self-trust and self-encouragement. That takes courage and a rather lovely kind of stubbornness, the seeds of which you must find above all "in the dark, in the unsayable and unconscious, in experiences unreachable by reason alone."

Again, the precious *how* you navigate this journey is not for Rilke to determine. Nor is it ours to "advise." *Stretching between birth and death, your life is much like every other life,* and *it is utterly specific, and certainly irreplaceable.* This dance between the known and unknown allows for spontaneity, for surprises—within and between us, as writers—and for you, as readers.

Everyday life is here in Rilke's writings as it needs to be. There's a rare sensuality and earthiness as well as a visionary wisdom rooted in Rilke's poems. There's pleasure here, too, as well as willingness to know the "more" that comes from the inwardness unique to the human mind. The freedoms Rilke understood and that we evoke here are not timid; they may even be radical. In the single novel he wrote, *The Notebooks of Malte Laurids Brigge,* he posed a series of questions about authenticity that cut against the grain of modern social conventions. At one point early in that book he asks:

> Is it possible that despite our discoveries and advances, despite our culture, religion, and science, *we have remained on the surface of life* [our italics]? Is it possible that even this surface, which might still have been something, has been covered with an incredibly tedious

material which makes it look like living-room furniture during the summer vacation?

Rilke answers his own questions: *Yes, it is possible.* In a later letter he put it this way: "My God, why do people live by conventions that pinch them like a too-tight costume, preventing them from discovering their invisible soul, that dancer among the far stars?"

We do not only "believe," we *know* it is possible for you to discover your soul, invisible but not imperceptible. It may even be your highest imperative to realize that you, too, are a "dancer among the far stars." And what is this but the moment when you decide, yes, to begin again—*now*? As Rilke wrote in an early journal entry:

> I love beginnings, despite the fear and uncertainty they bring. When I have won for myself a joy or reward, or when I wish that something had not happened, when I want to deny an experience the right to remain in my past—in such moments, I begin. And what do I do? *I simply begin* [our italics]. I've already begun a thousand lives like this. I feel as though a whole generation must come to fulfill all these lives so that they won't remain unfinished.... All the same, I am perhaps already in the process of having begun *my* life, the life none of us relinquishes until it's completed...

You may already have faced difficult and perhaps desperately unwelcome questions in your life. *How will I survive when...? Which way will I turn if...? Why does my beloved have to bear this unfair, unbearable suffering? Whom can I trust...? What will you think of me...? Can I go on?*

Beginnings are the pathway into a future that we share, one that is entirely yours. Whatever day this is, and however familiar your daily circumstances, *you have not lived this day before.* Injustices happen. Violence erupts on the political as well as the intimately personal levels. Tempests flare, inside and out. You are subject to unconscious drives. So are others around you. You also, wondrously, have the gift of consciousness, a capacity to become increasingly "awake." And, as you do, you begin to discover, with Rilke, that *you are the future.*

If you've come to a point in your life where you sense a yearning to see life in its mysterious immensity and beauty (as well, sometimes, as in its inevitable "terrors"), then Rilke might be the poet you need. Or perhaps it's not quite the "poet" who is needed. Rather, *it is your decision to live poetically,* which is to say, *spaciously.* That call to "live the questions" is just one of Rilke's many invitations into non-conformity of thinking and being.

These invitations are as relevant today as when he was writing. Maybe even more so. Who could have predicted the ubiquitousness of fundamentalisms, religious and otherwise, in so many parts of the 21st-century world? Or the harm they do as they cut us off from one another and the natural world?

> *Nothing was yet done before I beheld it,*
> and every becoming stood still;
> my ways of seeing are ripe, and, like a bride,
> to each one comes the thing each wills.
>
> *Nothing is too small for me, and I love it anyway...*

This is not an "easy" poem. It may not be one you instantly write out to make your own. But it places the poet and his readers center stage, pointing directly as it does to our relationships to things, events, experiences, nature, as well as people. We are more than social beings: *we are relational.* Whether this feels generally good or frequently uncomfortable depends on unconscious as well as conscious factors, which may reveal themselves to us only as *every becoming stood still...* Many of the deepest questions that may confuse, intimidate, or dismay us circle around relatedness: our desires for it, our hurts from it, our willingness (or not) to receive as well as give.

On one point, however, Rilke is unswervingly clear: we must live the questions for ourselves, not for others—nor can we presume that they can live them for *us*. The poet's invitations urge greater engagement and boldness of interest, far from indifference or barren cynicism. Living the questions, *your* questions, and not those of others, and living *into* these questions with heart and trust subdues the temptation to split off from ourselves or to split our experiences into a good/bad dichotomy that leaves us hiding from parts of our own experiences, turning from the source of our wisdom.

Here, especially, we need the courage to begin again, to stand still, if briefly—and to do so trusting in the wholeness that holds us, even—or perhaps especially—in the times when we believe we are fragmenting inwardly or falling fatally apart.

*

"Freedom is the only worthy goal in life. It is won by disregarding things that lie beyond our control." Those words are not from Rilke but from Epictetus, the Greek Stoic philosopher who urged against the obsessive nature of our contemporary belief that a single shift in circumstances will shift our wellbeing, "once and for all." Almost two thousand years ago, Epictetus advised: "A ship should not ride on a single anchor, nor life on a single hope." It was far closer to our "today" when Rilke wrote:

> Nothing is too small for me, and I love it anyway
> and paint it on the golden base and large—
> and hold it high; and I don't know *whose*
> soul this might yet free...

This means living into your life—your singular, astonishing life—with tolerance as well as curiosity and expansiveness. Tolerance doesn't mean putting up with whatever comes; it means accepting that on a crowded planet our urgent needs compete with the urgent needs of others, and resilience builds when "whatever comes" can be faced and lived at least somewhat skillfully. *You don't know whose soul this might yet free...*

Rilke suffered many setbacks, not always gracefully. We two writers have endured many setbacks, sometimes far from gracefully. But trust in a future comes not from the fall but from the rising. And from beginning—again. Not once. But many times. With some strength gained from a shift in expectation that is itself empowering, that liberates some of the frantic determination that things "must" be a certain way to be tolerable. Or the belief that you will be crushed or shattered if they are not.

The tolerance coming with this shift in attitude will markedly lessen your dread of things "going wrong." *Things will go wrong.* Things might also get better. *Things*—life, experiences, relationships—are always changing. A bigger view offers you the totality of *your own life* while also acknowledging how interconnected and interdependent we are: imaginatively, spiritually, and in our desires and longings.

*

Rilke's call and ours is not meant to make you a poet, at least not in any formal sense. More likely, it is a call *to find your poet's mind*, your seeker's heart, your innate appreciation of the world in which you find yourself, plus a sense of mystery and the immeasurable that goes beyond what you can see and touch, yet also animates those things.

Would that be his way of inviting you to live a *poetic* life, a life opened to the creative powers that flow in and through every life? And to dare to do this every day? And every night? To live a life in which you find the courage to risk beginning anew, again and again, despite your fears and uncertainties? And surely, in particular, in their presence? With Rilke, we dare to think so.

It is a summons to risk living into your *abundance* by discovering your struggles as the very place to start afresh. It is an invitation to be creative in your daily perceptions. As Rilke put it in a letter to a friend in the last years of his life:

> ...you cannot awaken often enough in this life *the sense of making a beginning within yourself.* There is so little

external change needed for that since we transform the world *from within our hearts* [our italics]. If the heart longs for nothing but to be new and expansive, the world is instantly the same as on the day of its creation and infinite.

To transform the world from within your heart: this conviction voices Rilke's deepest belief, not in some divine power that might act upon you, but in *your* discovery that you always carry within yourself the power to create and recreate when things fall apart. To begin again. And "hold high" what you have "painted" (imagined, created, made happen).

In the moment of this "starting afresh" and entering back into "this change," you'll sense that the creative flow of your life's work is happening not only within you, but through you. In the creativity of this change, in your risking to embrace the transformation of your life, you change nothing less than...the world. For you can—and will—"seize the forming day." *For you are the future.*

Let the dance begin.

CHAPTER 2

LIVING THE QUESTIONS

"Be patient toward all that is unresolved in your heart and try to love the questions themselves, like locked rooms and like books written in an utterly unknown language. Don't search now for the answers; they can't be given to you because you couldn't yet live them. And what matters is to live everything. Live the questions now. Perhaps on some future day you'll find yourself, slowly and imperceptibly, living into the answer."

—from *Letters to a Young Poet*

[*MARK S. BURROWS*]

In all the many remarkable books of poems Rilke published over the thirty-odd years of his writing career, his call to "love the questions" and "live [them] now" has become a commonplace. The phrase is so widely known, in fact, that many recognize it who have little or no familiarity with Rilke or his writings. Yet it captures something that goes to the depth of our yearning for inner spaciousness. For curiosity, and the freedom it suggests. Even for joy.

Originally written to a young writer who had sought his counsel and eventually published, after Rilke's death, as *Letters to a Young Poet*, the claim is a startling one. Rilke offered it not as a demand. The invitation to "live the questions" bears witness to the vast resource of inwardness we each carry, suggesting how we might tap into it.

It also stands as a needed corrective, voicing a counter-cultural challenge that has inspired readers over the generations since he first formulated it in a letter of 1903. It invites us to ponder the mysterious gift that is our life without trying to solve its difficulties, fix what feels broken, or complete what seems unfinished.

I first came upon this letter as a college student when I was also a young poet. At the time, I found Rilke's call to "be patient with what is unresolved in your heart" difficult to hear, but I sensed its power ringing true in the depths of my being. It seemed that Rilke's point was not simply that of offering gratuitous advice at that anxious place where the uncertainties of youth and young adulthood unsettle many of us. It had more to do with his conviction that if our dreams are to take form, we must open ourselves to the abundance of life, with all its complexities and contradictions. His poems and letters invite us to "love" the questions, to indwell what is unsettled in our lives and in our world.

Rilke's approach, as he reveals it in his writings and above all in his letters, rarely offered advice. He rather probed that depth within us that ancient philosophers spoke of as "soul," that spacious carrying-dimension of the "self" that grounds us. That shapes us in the heart of what he simply called our "innerness," beyond comprehension or explanation. Call it the shaping energy of a part of us that abides in the midst of what he spoke of as our "fleetingness." Call it the energy that is common to each of us, and distinctively singular as "ours." Call it the dimension of our lives that is transcendent, yet a part we only come to know in the immanence—that is, the immediacy and "hereness"—of our particular life.

His counsel in these letters—to us as to that young poet named Franz Kappus, a mere seven years his junior—is to face what is unsettled, unresolved, and unfinished within us. And to embrace it as the gateway through which we can begin to realize what it means to "live everything." With all our insufficiencies and brokenness. And to do so in this moment of our lives. This is what he means in his call to "live the questions now."

His encouragement is to face what might seem to us hidden and utterly inaccessible—like a locked book. Or, to update the metaphor, a portal for which we have no password. How can you be curious in the face of such an impasse? How can you remain open to wait and listen for what it might reveal to you over time in the face of your fears and against your expectations? How can you simply *be* in the midst of what is unresolved within you?

This was Rilke's advice, as poignant for us in the flush of youth with its often-contradictory energies as it is somewhere along the pathway of our later lives all the way to our elder years. Finding a way to be curious, to be open to the unknown, to be ready to be surprised is not the goal of life's journey. It *is* that journey itself. Such a notion is deeply counter-cultural in societies like ours, impatient in the rush to fix what is broken and ignore or evade what is difficult, intent on finding a "meaning" already anticipated or desired. Against this pressure, Rilke—following the philosopher Nietzsche, whom he had read when still himself a young poet—elevated the importance of not knowing. Of giving ourselves to an unknowing that opens us to a wisdom we could not have expected and may have ignored by another path.

*

After the intense years of his great love-affair with Lou Andreas-Salomé, Rilke left city-life in Berlin bound for Worpswede, a farming village located in the "Teufelsmoor" (Devil's Moor) about twenty miles from the city of Bremen. That region of Lower Saxony was a vast wetland of peat bogs that had been slowly drained over the generations as farmers dug canals, rendering the land arable, with a flat horizon as vast and open as the skies above.

Rilke, along with several dozen other young artists—among them writers, weavers, potters, painters, and furniture craftsmen—had sought out this quiet corner of Lower Saxony to form a community of shared work and conversation. This remarkable circle of artists included the painters Fritz Mackensen, Paula Modersohn-Becker and her husband Otto Modersohn, the sculptor Clara Westhoff who would become Rilke's wife, and the Jugendstil designer Heinrich Vogeler.

Many of them had met at the distinguished Art Academy in Düsseldorf but moved to this sparsely populated region to form an artist colony. This communal venture stood against the long-established tradition of artists choosing to live in the bustling cities of the time, gathering in salons hosted by wealthy patrons willing to support them and purchase their work. There, in a remote village far from the pressures of urban life, these artists sought to form a "common life" shaped by the creative energies of early socialism, one in which the practice of the arts formed a crucial foundation for their life together.

Rilke met Clara there, and after marrying they moved into a small cottage in nearby Westerwede where they brought their only child, Ruth, into the world. Their stay was to be a short one, interrupted the following year when Rilke, and later Clara, moved to Paris, leaving Ruth in the care of her parents in nearby Bremen.

At that time farmers still cut peat by hand, drying it to use as a source of heat for the long, cold winters, transporting it on small boats rigged with rust-colored sails along narrow canals formed to drain the bogs across the seemingly endless flat landscape. With its low-built, cross-timbered houses and barns, all still sheltered by thatched roofs, the village seemed to Rilke and his peers a haven from the industrialization that had turned the coal-mining region near Düsseldorf—Duisburg and Essen, Bochum and Dortmund—into an increasingly polluted and congested area along the Ruhr River.

Rural villages like Worpswede and nearby Westerwede seemed rooted in an unchanging past, nestled as they were at the time—and still are today—within the spacious horizons that stretched across the northern moors of East Friesland and beyond, to the North Sea. That wide landscape with its spacious skies had a shaping power on Rilke's imagination. It evoked within him a sense of possibility that shaped what he would later refer to as "the Open." In one of his *Letters to a Young Poet* Rilke described these surroundings with an affection bordering on devotion:

> Here, where a powerful landscape surrounds me over
> which the winds move from across the seas, here I feel

that no one can answer those questions and feelings
that, in their depths, take on a life of their own. For
even the most articulate among us are mistaken with
their words when they should gesture quietly toward
what is almost unsayable.

What are those "questions and feelings" Rilke is here referring to, that
"no one can answer"? Those problems that resist easy solutions or overly
facile explanations? He is not referring to the small things we often worry
about, those petty annoyances and little grievances that nag us. No, he
has in mind the larger, seemingly intractable questions that stir us in the
deep of the night: *Who am I, really? Why am I here? Am I a failure? What
should I make of my life? Is there a meaning strong enough to hold me through
the hard times?* These are the questions that often leave us mute, ones that
Rilke senses we would do better by simply "gesturing quietly" toward "what
is almost unsayable." And note well: not altogether, but "almost" unsayable.
Which is where poetry comes in and the arts find their place.

After living within that experimental community for a little more
than a year, however, Rilke left for Paris where he hoped to meet the
great sculptor Auguste Rodin, aided by a letter of introduction from
his wife. It turned out to be a difficult move. The city overwhelmed him
with its noise, its filth, and its commotion, a striking contrast from the
genial life that he had discovered in the remote village of Worpswede.
"Everything sounds different here," Rilke wrote of Paris, "drowned out
as it is by an excessive noise that makes everything tremble." Leaving
the city after his first prolonged stay there, "suffering and exhausted," he
returned to "the great northern plain [of Lower Saxony], whose wide-
ness and silence and skies," he hoped, would encourage his recovery.

Vast landscapes can have this effect upon us, which is one of the
reasons we find ourselves drawn to the spaciousness of an unimpeded
horizon. Whether the plains of the American Midwest that I came to
know as a boy, the vistas gained when summiting the mountains of New
Hampshire's White Mountains I explored during later years, or the
sense of an endless horizon along the sea where I now live in midcoast

Maine: all these have come to offer me, as the Teufelsmoor did for Rilke, that glimpse of "wideness and silence and skies" that somehow mirrors the soul's expansiveness. The sense of immensity, outer and inner, is part of what opens us to "live the questions" without seeking to solve the unsolvable or answer the unanswerable. It is this sense of what Rilke, late in his life, came to call "the Open" that encourages us to become content with what is "almost unsayable" in our lives.

Our "wellness," of course, can never depend upon geography only. As Rilke reminds us, the inner landscapes are also immensely important and not unconnected to the former. That interior solitude is where we might discover something like a song, one that we often ignore or cannot find in the hurried, worried lives that define our days—and nights. In an early journal entry, he expanded on this:

> Whether you are surrounded by the singing of a lamp
> or a storm's sounds, by the evening's breathing or the
> sighing of the sea, there is a vast melody of a thousand
> voices that never abandons you and only occasionally
> leaves room for your solo. To know when you have to
> join in, that is the secret of your solitude, just as it is the
> art of true human interaction: to let yourself take leave
> of the lofty words to join in with the one shared melody.

What spacious wisdom this suggests. The path of our longed-for healing, he here reminds us, comes from realizing that we belong to what he came to call "the Whole," however broken we might feel. The "secret of [our] solitude" calls us to join "with the one shared melody" that courses through this life, inviting us to "live everything." *Everything.*

*

Written more than a century ago in a letter included in a thin volume published posthumously, in 1929, with the unassuming title *Letters to a Young Poet*, Rilke's urging has lost nothing of its relevance and appeal.

On the contrary, the phrase "live the questions" speaks poignantly to those burdened by the pressures of late-modern societies in the West, weighted as they are with exhausted certainties, hollow presumptions, and the inner longings these evoke for many. Amid the marketers of our day with their slick techniques, something deep within us recognizes the truth in Rilke's claim that what matters most is *living* things—indeed, living *everything*, as the poet suggests.

Something within us senses the truth of this call. How might we live the questions and honor what is unresolved within us? In another of these letters, he put it this way:

> I think that you will not have to remain without a solution if you trust in things that are like the ones my eyes are now resting upon. If you trust in nature, in what is simple in nature, in the small things that hardly anyone sees and that can so suddenly become huge, immeasurable; if you have this love for what is humble and try very simply, as someone who serves, to win the confidence of what seems poor: then everything will become easier for you, more coherent and somehow more reconciling, not in your conscious mind perhaps, which stays behind, astonished, but in your innermost awareness, awakeness, and knowledge.

This is not to suggest that Rilke was ever entirely or even relatively free of what he once called our "beautiful anxieties." Far from this, he seemed particularly keen on acknowledging the role that confusion plays in opening us to the widening inner horizons that carry us. To the end of his life, he also faced the worrisome burdens of fragile health, financial strain, and relational difficulties—including those of his marriage and family. He also suffered from an undercurrent of existential angst about his place in the world, both the physical and social "worlds" he inhabited in fin-de-siècle Europe and the decades that followed and those that he faced as a poet and artist.

Should this diminish our interest in him? Or distance us from his ideas? I would say not. We turn to Rilke as a poet, not as a spiritual teacher or a prophet. We learn from his struggles to remain true to his creative calling. It is the recognizable paradoxes and complexities in the man, which we know in our own lives, that make his sometimes-sublime insights of such interest. He knew failure and struggle first-hand—his own, which anticipate ours as well.

*

My earliest encounter with Rilke was when I was a student in Munich, Germany, a city that became familiar to Rilke during the final decades of his life. I had come upon a copy of an early edition of *Briefe an einen jungen Dichter*—or *Letters to a Young Poet*—in a small antiquarian bookstore in Munich, the city where Rilke occasionally lived and briefly studied during his early life, and the place he returned to after the end of the First World War.

After perusing the first letter I found myself utterly absorbed by the probing nature of his writing voice and bought it. That encounter began what has been a lifelong journey with this small collection and, over time, with the wider arc of his poems and writings. I'd immediately noticed the inscription on the inside cover, written in an elegant cursive hand with a fountain pen: "*Weihnachten* (Christmas) *1955, E. S.*" It was surely coincidental that this happened to be the year of my first Christmas as an infant, but it seemed at the time to point to a mysterious synchronicity.

I have no idea who "E. S." was, and will never know why they might have selected this volume—or given it as a gift to an unnamed recipient. What I do remember is that after finding it, I found my way to a cozy café just off the city's central "Hay Market Square," and read it straight through—with many interruptions and numerous long entries in my journal—in a single sitting. From the outset I found myself drawn by the authenticity and urgency of Rilke's voice, which seemed to be addressing me directly as if he knew my questions and understood the disordered shape of my confusions.

Over the decades that followed, I have returned to it more times than I can remember, finding in the wisdom Rilke there imparts insight, solace, encouragement, and, often enough, direction. Millions of other readers in German as well as those finding it in the more than a dozen other languages into which it has been translated have shared that experience. Despite the passage of time, Rilke's musings have if anything gained in the relevance with which they probe the depths of cultural crisis and change we face in late modernity.

Rilke voiced his call to "live the questions" to encourage an aspiring young poet, urging him to *live first* and see if poems would come later from the depth of that creative engagement. *Live into the depths of your life, and only then consider whether to write*, Rilke counseled:

> You look to the surfaces, and this is what you should by all means avoid doing. No one can give you advice or help you. No one. There is only one thing to do: *Go into yourself*. Explore the reason why you feel the need to write; see whether its roots reach into the deepest depths of your heart.

Rilke's correspondence with this young man began in the fall of 1902 when Kappus sent a selection of his poems to then twenty-six-year-old Rilke, already an established writer of growing acclaim. In a letter accompanying them, Kappus asked whether he had a "vocation" as a poet, and if he should pursue writing as a profession. Did he have what it took?

In the response that young Mr. Kappus received to this letter, Rilke addressed this question directly, and in ten letters that followed over the next six years he explored with his young counterpart the perennial questions we face: the nature of life and death; love and loss; sex and solitude; and—writing as the extraordinary, unconventional poet and person he was—he did so in a timeless and universal way. The great wisdom of his advice, though, was his reminder that if we hope to come to our senses, we must move beyond the surface of things, probing all the way to "the deepest depths" of the heart in our search to know what these questions call forth within us.

*

We live, as Rilke did, in a culture that distances us from each other, from the natural world, and, ultimately, from our very selves. We find our-selves saturated by its demands and by the pressures of a 24/7 society. The "disenchantment of the world" is how the German sociologist Max Weber described our plight. Writing in 1919, he lamented that ours was an age "characterized by rationalization and intellectualization, and above all by *the disenchantment of the world*. Its resulting fate is that pre-cisely the ultimate and most sublime values have withdrawn from public life." How true this was in Rilke's day, and, if in different ways, in ours.

What are those "ultimate and most sublime values"? An openness to mystery; a sense that the invisible forces that seek to be at work in shap-ing us should not be rationalized and cannot be controlled; a valuing of community by which we know that we somehow belong to each other, in the midst of our differences; a sense that we belong to the communities of this earth; the inviolable sanctity of nature of which we are an integral part—but not the center, and never the whole. Weber, with Rilke, recog-nized the erosion of such values as constituting the malaise of "modern" societies, leaving us fearful, alienated from nature and from our own nat-ural connectedness—to the earth, to each other, and to our true nature. This leaves us, he felt—as Rilke had suggested several decades earlier in *Letters*—feeling isolated and exposed.

In such times, Rilke's insistence that "it is always the question of the 'whole' with which we are concerned" is likely to strike something within us that we know to be true, even if it seems far from an easy reach. He knew this, too, going on to say that "this 'whole,' even when we grasp it in a rush of happiness or an act of pure will, is interrupted by the fool-ishness, mistakes, shortcomings, and pernicious intentions that come between us, and by what is helpless and dark—yes, by nearly everything that engages us daily." We sense this, you and I, in the exhaustion that overcomes us in our harried lives. We know that we, too, must move beyond the surfaces of things, opening ourselves to the "deepest depths of the heart" on which our lives depend.

*

The journey Rilke invites us on begins where each of us *is* in our lives, not where we think we *ought to be*. It has to do with discovering our deeper, emerging self at the heart of our questions. The "I" who is often a mystery to us, first of all, the one who is unfinished, changing, becoming. Our living into what is "almost unsayable," what draws us to the wisdom held in poems like Rilke's, is what beckons us to open ourselves to the truth of who we already *are*, of who we are *becoming*, not some presumed self we might wish to be.

Why turn to a poet to make sense of your life? What might poetry have to do with accompanying you as you find your way home to who you truly are, in your deepest nature? Could it be possible that a poet like Rilke could help you discover your path into wholeness which an ancient Hebrew text distilled into a simple phrase: "Choose life, so that you and your descendants may live" (Deuteronomy 30:19)?

For Rilke, everything depends on this primary act of choice. Each of us, with gifts of awareness, is free to choose what is life-giving. My own discovery of this truth as a young adult was initially disconcerting, and only little by little did it become engaging and even thrilling. While I sensed the truth rooted in Rilke's call to "live the questions," I felt strongly drawn, as most of us do in these formative years, toward answers that might secure my future. In the anguish of that struggle at the heart of what felt like my divided soul, I found myself caught between the aspirations of a professional career as an academic and what had become the irresistible lure of poetry. Like most people, I needed to make a living, to function in a material world: the outer world did and does matter as well as the inner one. And the enormous privilege of having any sense of "choice" was not lost on me then. But I realized that the poet's call was not simply a hobby or an avocation.

In the process I came to sense that the "outer" world of the academy was not enough to meet my heart's hunger. Against the pressures of wanting to build a solid career, with all its securities, I wondered if I could heed Rilke's call to give myself to the substance of my everyday life and make *this* the subject of my work. "Describe your sorrows and desires," he advised, "your drifting thoughts and your belief in some sort of beauty." That summons shook me when I first read it, and it has not let me go since. It is the heart of what it means *to live your questions*. And this refusal to seek premature answers, to dwell in the wisdom we encounter in our uncertainties, is the surest path to discover our "belief in some sort of beauty."

This is not to suggest that you or I choose what is life-giving for our own sake alone. You are not an island in some far-off ocean, even when you might feel the weighty burden of your solitude, with all its aloneness. No, you and I are part of the great mystery of the "whole" to which we belong—and which belongs *to us*. This is a lived understanding common to the world's mystical traditions, in and beyond those of religion. It is this intuition that summons us to embrace life's "enchantment," aware of whatever seems to work against it. Perhaps especially this. This sense of belonging does not require you to affirm fixed ideas or accept imposed beliefs. In fact, it is—like the greatest truths—learned amid all those interruptions that you endure like burdens.

Sometimes, though, we come to sense this belonging most acutely in its absence: when we feel we do not belong. When we let outside pressures define and limit the arc of our desires. Then something in our outer or inner worlds turns on its axis, not necessarily because we have willed it, and we find that we somehow belong to what Rilke often referred to simply as "the Whole." That we are *alive*, with an inexhaustible fullness of being. That we find ourselves summoned to *live the questions*. Ours, however awkward or demanding these might be. And to begin to do this here and now.

*

Living the questions does not mean abandoning self-inquiry. On the contrary, it means deepening it. It means seeking the inner space you need to embrace your life *as it is*, the interruptions along with the conflicts and confusions you face, and to do so with deepening trust and hard-won self-respect.

Only with "patience toward everything that is unresolved within your heart" can you begin to grasp what Rilke means in urging us to "live the questions." Which is one way of saying, to affirm the life you *have*, with all its unavoidable challenges. This calls on patience, curiosity, and self-trust, qualities we repeatedly evoke in these pages. "Bringing them to mind," to consciousness, is a powerful act of self-respect and self-healing. This takes courage and promises to guide us toward the sense of belonging we long to know.

When you set out to follow this path, you will slowly begin to discover that this way of being opens you to how others belong, with you, to "the Whole," with their questions and doubts, fears and uncertainties—as well as their gifts and joys. You'll begin to know yourself woven into the web of interconnectedness, of "interbeing," as the late Zen master, poet, and teacher of peace, Thich Nhat Hahn, often put it.

If you wonder about how to do this, you'll find yourself in the company of most of those who are around you, however confident they might appear to be. Rilke is quite blunt on this point. And here he draws on a strange, unexpected image—he is a poet, after all, and "thinks" in images, which reach to the deepest part of our creative mind. At first glance, this image is one that might not make sense to you. "Cherish the questions as if they were locked rooms or books written in a language you cannot understand." Reading such advice, you might be confused or even distressed. For when you find yourself overwhelmed with things, facing an insurmountable problem or stuck in some "dead end" that seems inescapable, the last thing you want is to have someone tell you to "cherish the questions" that seem so central to your discontent.

In an acutely anxious age like ours, we find ourselves surrounded by those with solutions on offer. Anxiety has become a mega-business. What sense could there be, then, in having someone tell you to approach this as if trying to enter a room that is sealed off? Or to linger with a book written in a language indecipherable to you?

What at first appears to be an insurmountable obstacle can reveal itself slowly as a way forward. These images, though seeming at first glance ridiculous, might well guide you through the impasses in your life. For even if you were to find some magical pill, acquire more confidence, find a "perfect" mate/job/passion, make all the right connections for your loved ones, even saving them from grief, what then?

*

What if Rilke is reminding you that your life—which is yours alone to explore—calls you to acknowledge, not avoid, what is unresolved in this world and, yes, in your own life? And that through quiet, patient inwardness you might discover something of the truth of your "one wild and precious life," as poet Mary Oliver hails it, not as a solution to these problems but as a path through what is and may well remain unsettled?

How reassuring might it be, too, to discover the naturalness of doing this *without* seeking a once-and-for-all solution? Rilke's call to cherish the questions is, at its heart, a call to be patient with yourself, so that you might begin to understand who you *are* rather than rushing in to decide what you should *do*. It is a call to you. And to me. Writing this today, I affirm my own listening into what is unresolved in my own life, and I find that, little by little, I am enlarged by this discovery.

His "cherishing" image reminds us that little that we might try outside ourselves will get to the heart of the matter. For the matter of the heart is where our deep identity lies—often hidden from us, even though it is in plain sight. Your life and mine, woven into the fabric of an interconnectedness we can hardly imagine, much less experience. In this very moment of your reading and living, the poet is urging you to see your life as an unfolding journey, one laced with joys and enchantments alongside what often appear to be—and sometimes are—insoluble burdens and intractable absurdities. And, for that very reason, one that seems fraught with challenges you must learn to face with minimal judgment or blame, of yourself or others.

When Rilke reminded his young correspondent that "…it finally comes down to this: to live everything. *Live* the questions now. Perhaps on some future day you'll find yourself, slowly and unknowingly, living into the answer," he went on to add: "Perhaps you already carry within yourself the possibility to create and shape—as a particularly sacred and pure way of living." Your wisdom, too, is unfolding, even more so when you allow yourself to pause, reflect, and consider familiar things from an unfamiliar and more spacious perspective. This is how self-knowledge accumulates within you and radiates outward toward others.

This is also how such knowing begins to remake you, steadying you, first, from within. Only then does it open you toward others when you begin to find that what is unresolved within you is something you share with others, that together you belong with "them" to the world you imagined was *beyond* but slowly began to discover *within* your own heart through the inwardness we are creating which holds us—with all else— together. Along this path, you will begin to find yourself, with others, as an inviolable part of "the Whole," a discovery that invites you to "live everything."

CHAPTER 3

HOW DO OTHERS SEE YOU?

O you tender ones, now and then step out
into the breath that isn't about you;
let it part around your cheeks,
and then join again, trembling, behind you.

O you who are blessed, o you who are whole,
who appear to be the origin of hearts.
Bows for the arrows and the arrows' targets,
your tear-soaked smile shines beyond forever.

Don't fear suffering, and give the burdens
back to the earth's weight;
heavy are the mountains, heavy the seas.

Even the trees you planted as children
became too heavy long ago; you couldn't carry them.
But the winds . . . but the spaces . . . .

—*The Sonnets to Orpheus* I.4

[*STEPHANIE DOWRICK*]

The torrent of creativity that allowed *The Sonnets to Orpheus* to move from the poet's mind to his pages is virtually unmatched in Rilke's time, or ours. Translator and scholar Edward Snow makes the claim: "This is surely the most astonishing burst of inspiration in the history of litera-ture." After writing them, Rilke wrote to his publisher, "Dear friend, now I can breathe again…"

Breathing is our most fundamental experience, as it is for all spe-cies. It is our species alone, however, for whom breathing—and all that breath allows—becomes conscious, something to wonder about, while also being entirely natural. Perhaps that sums up what Rilke offers?

Is this sonnet a call to the intrinsic belonging that breath brings? I'm not sure. Nor do I need to be *sure*. Because Rilke is demonstrat-ing immediacy plus transitoriness, as well as the profundity of *being breathed*, of *being breath* as breath parts around us, while animating every cell within us.

This invitation to be at once more conscious and far less *self*-con-scious offers an exquisite paradox. It goes to the heart of what deepening perception can offer. You and I are, at this very moment, both the person we are and the person we are perceived to be, though this is itself never static. Transitoriness. Immediacy. *How do others see you?*

It is exactly this kind of teasing paradox that works as an exuberant key to liberation for some. And as a tormenting frustration for others. So, let's bring it to the ground of one of the biggest, deepest, most mean-ingful inner questions of all: *How do others see me?* And not far behind: *How close does this come to the way I see myself? Or want to be seen? Am I seen only in my roles, my professional identity, through my relatedness to others? Am I captured by a national or religious identity that may or may not fit? And where in all this is my most private self, the "all" of who I am?*

It may be only yesterday that you asked yourself how you were being seen by another person, or a group of people. Or by someone you partic-ularly admire. This kind of self-questioning is common, and commonly the trigger for self-doubt, or chronic anxiety. "Seeing," after all, may be an all-encompassing word for perceiving, weighing up, judging. For you now though, does it speak most poignantly to the self you curate for the world? Or to the "you" that few know?

When it comes to understanding *how we see others*, this may be a more familiar process. It happens automatically—unless we pause to check how close to or how far off the mark our assumptions are. After all, the more familiar our habitual assumptions, the more convincing they will seem to us. When it comes to our own selves though, many of us live with a longing to be seen beyond that fleeting glance—*and with a fear of exactly that. Would you love me if you knew me in all my complexity?* Ours is a world where "deep seeing" in any sphere is rare. Dismissive stereotyping abounds, routinely diminishing others'—if not our own—very humanity.

Yet despite recognizing what's going on, it is still all too easy to attribute power to others to perceive and judge our *vulnerability*. Or our self-worth. Status anxiety is everywhere in the so-called advanced nations, based on commercial coercion and exploitation. We may even be chronically attuned to a belief that others' view of us has more weight than our own self-knowledge. This makes us highly sensitive to anything that hints of criticism, and distrustful of what may be appreciative or praising. Those real or imagined criticisms may even match the harsh way we talk to ourselves. *We want reassurance; we disbelieve reassurance. We want to be met; we fear being met.* Can a poet—an authentically complex poet—illuminate this?

> O you tender ones, now and then step out
> into the breath that isn't about you;
> let it part around your cheeks,
> and then join again, trembling, behind you.

Breath that is more than your own: vision—including of your magnificent self—that is more than the material world has to offer? Yes.

You and I are inevitably conditioned by reductive thinking that's culturally embedded. We belong to time, place, even in the nature of our small rebellions. We confuse what is familiar with what is "correct", the "right way" or "normal"; but to whom? Reading widely is an antidote to this; so is travel; so is learning to interrogate your assumptions. I've never much liked Rilke's famous poem, "The Panther," often the one poem of his that German school students learn. But there is brutal truth in it of the agonies of confinement, including the confinement of a closed mind. Speaking of the panther, pacing in the prison of his zoo cage, Rilke wrote:

> His gaze, from pacing behind the bars,
> has grown so weary that it sees nothing more.
> It seems to him like a thousand bars,
> with no world at all beyond them.

Conventionality confines us. A dulling of our innate creativity or curiosity diminishes us. But on the page? In the presence of a true poet? Ah! That's where freedom flourishes. Or can.

*

When, as a committed reader, you meet a writer on the page and feel "met" in return, or in some real way better understood, there is a relief there that's almost beyond words. It can make you feel less alone. It may make sense of your inchoate yearnings. It may even assuage those inward questions, "*Is it all right to be who I am? Does my life make sense? Does my life have intrinsic meaning?*"

Meeting someone through their writing can be a peculiarly intimate experience. You can "take in" what you need. You can make that writer "yours," even while knowing other readers may be making their different—or perhaps not so different—claims.

…Bows for the arrows and the arrows' targets…

At once, *this*. At the same time, *that*. For passionate readers, a sense of inward "meeting" is likely. We read with and through our emotions and instincts as much as with and through our intellect. We might also attribute a depth of wisdom to a favorite writer who is there on the page but would be difficult to locate in everyday conversation—or in what we casually call "real life."

Yet what's received from the page is *real.* It involves the imagination and consciousness, as much as it does the conjuring up of idealizations and projections. This is why we can feel almost laughably possessive about the writers we care about most, even while we may remain eager to share our enthusiasm with others.

Writers themselves are not immune from these processes. Indeed, there were several writers and artists thoroughly idealized by Rilke at different points in his writing life. French sculptor Auguste Rodin and the painter Paul Cézanne were among them, also the poet Paul Valéry whose work Rilke eagerly translated from its original French late in his life. This kind of projection can be stirring. It echoes the idealizations of romantic love where—usually for a limited time only—you believe you are at last seen at your best. The anxiety of *How do others see me?* may be briefly assuaged.

You may think of your writer-idealizations as unilateral rather than relational, as with a lover, yet I'd hazard it's never quite that definite. After all, you are responding on the page not to a romantic projection but to words, concepts, images that have somehow allowed you to feel "seen." Understood. Or more vibrantly alive. Such *inter-connectedness* between writers and readers matters. It's what reading allows. It's what reading gives. It's what writers and writing need.

Some readers picking up this book will have done so because they are already drawn to the "greatest lyric poet of the 20th century," the one often described as the "poet of inner spaces," and feel, across time, somehow understood by him. They may feel an identification, not least with his refusals to be confined by stifling conventions. From his own "inner spaces" Rilke speaks to ours. Better still, he does this not by taking himself off to the top of a mountain or sitting at the mouth of a cave, but from the messy, ambiguous, sometimes-glorious, sometimes-desperate bundle of experiences we call ordinary life. Rilke is one of us who is simultaneously not one of us.

*

In the English-language world, Rilke is rivaled in popularity with readers only by the 13th-century Sufi poet Rumi. Both these wildly different but equally mesmerizing writers have an appeal that extends beyond committed readers or those seeking an inclusive spiritual perspective. Their freeing, startling words—in better and also in not-so-good translations—find their way into movies, plays, and multiple cultural references. Their words are frequently evoked when a gathering needs the solemnity of an "occasion." Or to express a rejoicing that could otherwise only come from music.

Does that mean, though, that you would be keen to sit down with Rilke, given time-travel and half a chance? To let him know you as a specific person, not just "another reader"? What would the prospect feel like of *being seen* by this slender, soft-spoken, dapper, punctilious (some say fussy) man? By a writer like Rilke, a vegetarian who avoided alcohol, who was reputed to be a gifted conversationalist and a charming and sometimes generous host, yet even better known for his unwavering need for what he called "limitless solitude"? Would you feel yourself *worthy* of taking up his time? Most crucially, do you sense you would get more from an hour or so of time with the poet than you might from reading—at your own pace and in your own time—the poems and letters he left in such abundance?

The attractions of "being with" another and of being seen in person are powerful. Our physicality is infinitely precious to who we are and how we relate to others. We tend to judge as well as be judged on appearances. Where is it, though, that you would more likely meet the "truer" Rilke? Conversing in French or German, formal in either language? Or on the page, where his vast vision is yours to pierce? As Rilke has been dead since 1926—at the age of 51—these are self-evidently hypothetical questions. We also cannot forget that even when alive many of his most intimate thoughts were conveyed on paper. In his writing, he could hold onto his much-needed solitude, while stretching out toward another.

Rilke's gift for an intimacy born from solitude was remarkable in his lifetime. In our age of instant communication, laden with curated versions of ourselves, it becomes even more exceptional. Rilke's poetry and letters sing of passionate connections, yet while he also knew loneliness, the shadow of solitude, he preferred aloneness and even loneliness to being presented with expectations he could not or would not willingly meet. On the page, *he could control how he was seen.* As all writers can. His famed words about solitude do not entirely mask his ever-present fears of closeness becoming overwhelming.

Those paradoxes may be ours, too. They let us—a hundred years later—feel (not just *acknowledge*) the contradictions in Rilke, on and off the page. In many translations into English this is ironed out. Yet it is Rilke's embrace of paradox and ambiguity, plus his refusal to tame life's greatest mysteries, that enables us to accept the fluctuations and contradictions in our own perceptions.

> O you tender ones, now and then *step out*
> *into the breath that isn't about you;*
> let it part around your cheeks,
> and then join again, trembling, behind you.

For all that, is Rilke someone I would want to walk through my front door, to be seen by as well as seeing? I am not sure. My preference for a personal encounter—if that were possible—might be for the company of Lou Andreas-Salomé, the German-Russian writer and eventual psychoanalyst, Rilke's first great love to whom he was most devoted to the very end. She was the woman Sigmund Freud called the "cleverest in Europe." Lou also wrote—fiction as well as essays and treatises on religion, culture, and psychology—and while her writing remains of interest, it doesn't leap from the page as Rilke's does. Yet her qualities of *presence* must surely have been magnetic. In a typically yearning letter Rilke wrote to her in August 1904, he displays his need, as well as admiration:

> I think of you, even though my thoughts don't know
> where to find you. I search for you in this great storm,

which fills the old trees of the park and throws light and
shadow across the paths and toward evening towers sky
upon sky over the meadows.

As a *person*, Lou was likely no less intellectually daunting than Rilke.
Nonetheless, she strikes me as more readily *seen*, and not only because
of her gender. "Time with Lou" was a more robust affair, I suspect, than
anxiously sharpening one's puny wit in Rilke's presence. The more I con-
jure up Rilke the person, the more confident I am that his *preference* was
to be met on the page. That's manageable intimacy, for the poet as much
as for his readers.

   We know that Rilke's comprehension of the Big Questions (and his
living into them) is profound. But of the two, it is more likely Lou who
would have been curious about the singular "you" who is each of us. Yet
when those honeyed hours were over, where might I turn for a depth of
thinking that's both consistently insightful (*einsichtig*) and far-sighted
(*weitsichtig*)? Having circled around a variety of possibilities I return not
to the fascinating Lou, but to the liberating invitation that's found within
Rilke's sonnet, dedicated to Orpheus, son of the Greek god Apollo, him-
self a musician, poet, and ardent lover. Quietening my own mind, I listen:

> Even the trees you planted as children
> became too heavy long ago; you couldn't carry them.
> But the winds . . . but the spaces . . . .

Years after their love affair in its most intense phases had ended, a late-
30s Rainer—a name he chose over his baptismal name, "René," at Lou's
urging—was writing to Lou. It was a European January day, freezing
we can imagine. As he often did, Rilke headed his letter with a location
note: "Duino near Nabresina, Austrian Littoral." His words are tender,
vulnerable:

> . . .I have been alone again only a few days, am now at
> last thanking you for your good letter. I have, you may

believe me, read much between the words, I walked up
and down in the garden with it as with something that
one wants to learn by heart, what would I do without
this voice: yours? I cannot tell you how intimate and
comforting it was to me, I am the lone little ant that has
lost its head, but you see the anthill and assure me it is
intact, and I will find my way into it again and make
myself useful.

What would I do without this voice: yours? Seen—really seen, and ide-
ally seen through the eyes of respect and affection—we feel ourselves
affirmed. Infants cannot survive without this. Adults barely can. *What
would I do without this voice: yours?*

The weight of these words is best understood by knowing that René
Karl Wilhelm Johann Josef Maria Rilke—his given birthname—was an
exceptionally lonely child, burdened by the misery of his pious, fraught,
socially insecure mother who continued to mourn a dead daughter long
after her son was born. And, as well, by the military expectations of a
kindly, ineffectual father whose professional under-achievements were
despised by his wife and whose ideas of masculinity could never be met
by his precocious son.

Until he met Lou in his early 20s, Rilke received neither the intel-
lectual nor emotional care he needed. Even then, his ardent longings
could not be fully met by the older, more sophisticated and worldly Lou.
Many love affairs would follow, some largely confined to letter writing,
as well as an early marriage to the pioneering sculptor and feminist,
Clara Westhoff, with whom he would have a daughter, Ruth. I find this
outpouring from Rilke to Lou a brave, moving acknowledgment of how
fundamentally we humans are sustained by relatedness: by the care of
others—and by giving care *to* others.

That simple proposition goes to the heart of so many of our dilem-
mas. But there's something else here that I love. And that embraces us
as *readers*. "I have, you may believe me, read much between the words; I
walked up and down in the garden with it as with something that one

wants to learn by heart. What would I do without this voice: yours? I cannot tell you how intimate and comforting it was to me."

I am struck by Rilke acknowledging Lou's "good letter" and that he has, taking the letter into himself, "read much between the words." He has in fact taken in, and into himself, the nourishment a "good letter" can bring. He has not rejected it, nor judged himself as unworthy. He hasn't mistrusted it, nor mistrusted Lou or Lou's sincerity in writing it. This is what we do when we make something of what we are reading: when we make it our own.

*

An imagined life is both more and far less than a still-unfolding "real" one where unconscious drives can still surprise us. Writing and reading reveal some of this. Both activities take us beyond intellect, beyond self-consciousness to a place of reverie: that state of mind that is neither thinking nor not-thinking. I would say this is where our creative forces wait. Post-Jungian scholar and poet, Robert Romanyshyn, puts it like this in his book, *The Wounded Researcher:* "In reverie, we are in that middle place between waking and dreaming, and, in that landscape, the borders and edges of a work become less rigid and distinct. They melt somewhat, and the work becomes a porous membrane through which the ancestors might slip into the work."

Hiding ourselves from ourselves generates chronic tension. So does second-guessing about how others not just see us but whether they accept us (or we them). Does this matter? There are aspects of Rilke's personal life that trouble me, perhaps especially a ruthlessness in preserving his gifts that apparently superseded any notion of obligation or desire to be with his wife and child, other than fleetingly. Yet my self-righteous judgments soften if I consider with what difficulty René Rilke emerged from the stultifying demands of an anguished, mourning mother who dressed him as a girl until he was four or five. Then there was the torment, as he later described it, that Rilke endured as a fragile, bullied boy at a strict military academy. That hurt plus seeming heartlessness remain with the

"Rilke" we meet on the page. But it is also mediated there—which is what art allows. It becomes:

> O you who are blessed, o you who are whole,
> who appear to be the origin of hearts.
> Bows for the arrows and the arrows' targets,
> your tear-soaked smile shines beyond forever.
>
> Don't fear suffering, and give the burdens
> back to the earth's weight;
> heavy are the mountains, heavy the seas.
>
> Even the trees you planted as children
> became too heavy long ago; you couldn't carry them.
> But the winds . . . but the spaces . . . .

This is not a process of transcendence, or not this only; it is a process of *transformation*. It is not something that happens within the writer alone, either. It is a process available to and within each reader. It involves surrender and receptivity, none of it passive. That, surely, is the alchemy of reading/writing and writing/reading. It is the song being sung. It is *us* singing. It is *us* being sung. As Rilke reminds us in an early poem from *The Book of Hours*, "...the song remains, beautiful."

Years after that letter to Lou, and only three years before his death, Rilke was writing to another of his lovers whom he called "Merline." Baladine Klossowska, a German-Jewish painter, born in Poland, dying in France in 1969, was also the mother of a son who became the famed painter, Balthus (1908–2001). Some of these love letters are aimed at keeping Merline at a distance that he, Rilke, believed he needed to preserve his artistic creativity. Yet their love affair initially rescued Rilke from a long period of depression and self-doubt, worsened by the immense distress he felt following the unspeakable horrors of the First World War. Baladine's devotion together with her own artistic gifts were significant in supporting Rilke to recover his poetic voice after a prolonged dry spell that had deeply dismayed him. He did not stop writing during that time, neither poetry nor letters, but work that exalted him, that he felt "given" to him, was, during those years, most painfully elusive.

The utter catastrophe that was the First World War had devastated any illusions that the world was becoming a "better place" or that the "cultured" societies of Europe were somehow above the cruelest and most protracted violence—a fact long known in every colonized nation. It was hideous for a man who, as a child, had loathed the hypocrisy of his military-style education, who despised and feared the rigid identity that nationalism insists upon, who spoke up for peace, and saw himself not as Austrian, Bohemian, or German, but as *European*.

Merline gave Rilke a genuine sense of "home" when she joined him in what was known as "Château de Muzot," a small tower-like castle in the Valais canton in Switzerland. This sense of *Heimatgefühl*, or "being-at-home," wouldn't last. Nonetheless, Rilke's two supreme collections, *Duino Elegies* and *The Sonnets to Orpheus*—quoted here—also emerged during the turbulent but rich "Merline years." Switzerland itself became a haven. In *Global Geneva*, Peter Hulm writes: "When [Rilke] made his first public appearance in Zurich in October 1919, an audience of 600 people turned out for his poetry reading."

Donald Prater, a later biographer, adds that "for all his tendency to disparage the Swiss and the artificial beauties of their country, he was learning to appreciate the virtues of a solid and regulated bourgeois existence he had never known; and it was dawning on him that this multinational and multilingual society might offer the lifeline he needed."

When Rilke wrote the words that follow to Merline, it had been years since a young, determined poet had fallen in love with Lou, changed his first name (at her urging) from René to Rainer, changed his handwriting to the more distinctive and elegant style Lou preferred—and, arguably, changed his expectations of himself.

It was also many years since the French sculptor August Rodin had insisted that a naïve, precocious Rilke begin to understand that art of any form required "work, work, always work"—in other words, less self-indulgence, and far more effort. Years, too, since Rilke had written what became his famous letters to an even younger poet, published post-humously as *Letters to a Young Poet*, letters in which Rilke wrote of *living the questions*.

Rilke's letter to Merline celebrates the moment that lifted him from the long drought he had endured; the moment that gave birth to the completion of the *Elegies* in February 1922, and the grand rush of the *Sonnets* that came so unexpectedly as he was finishing the *Elegies*. Questions that Rilke had no choice but to *live into* had been immense. They went to the very heart of his identity that was "poet" above all. But what is a poet when inspiration seems to have folded its wings, or stepped away, as happened to Rilke during the war years and those that followed? On a February evening in 1922, Rilke could say:

> Merline, I'm saved! The thing that weighed upon me and frightened me the most is done, and gloriously, I believe. It only took a few days, but I have never gone through such a hurricane of the heart and mind. I am still trembling from it—last night I thought I was going under; but there it is, I've conquered...From now on work will be smooth, stable, day-to-day, sure,—which will seem like a dead calm after this divine tempest, too great for anyone whomsoever. I can't write. But you will think it enough to have this good news. Give me your own. Dearest, dear, dear friend...

"I'm saved," is a burst of gratitude that moves me. What, after all, is "inspiration"? Where does it come from? How do we—or can we—ready ourselves to receive it? What is it that influences the tides within our thinking, or the tenor of our emotional responses?

You or I may have all the determination our human nature can bring. We may have the strongest possible desire to write "well," "originally," or even "wonderfully." Yet acts of will and determination alone are seldom enough. Perhaps a surrender to what is less personal, less conscious, more inwardly led as in dreams and reverie, is needed. Rilke's remark "From now on work will be smooth, stable, day-to-day, sure..." is also strikingly poignant in its human aspiration for a steady predictability that is far from realizable, except fleetingly.

The sonnet inspiring this chapter speaks to a greater truth and offers something closely akin to the moment-by-moment courage needed to live consciously and appreciatively: "Step out into breath that is more than your own" is the boldest of invitations. "Breath," "the air," "spaces," have no borders, boundaries, or constructed hierarchies of specialness, belonging, or exclusion. Air can be polluted, yes, but it cannot be hoarded. Or owned. We share the air that unites us. Breath sustains us.

In the celebrated cult movie, *JoJo Rabbit*, directed by Māori actor and Academy award-winning filmmaker, Taika Waititi, you might have heard these astonishing words from Rilke: "Let everything happen to you / beauty and terror. Just keep going, / no feeling is final." (You'll find our translation of the complete poem in the Introduction; each line sings.) How powerfully, though, that sentiment—conveyed in so few words—turns our attention forward, reminding us that seeing as well as being seen are momentary experiences: nothing fixed, as changeable as every other aspect of life.

Accepting this, can we, the poem asks, can *you*, afford a little more lightness of heart, vision, judgment? Can we, can *you*, trust living into that kind of inner and outer spaciousness where change is inevitable and nothing is fixed? Can you dare to know that *you are the future*?

In that same poem we are encouraged to "go to the edge of [our] longing..." The line evokes boldness; everything is in flux. It is your choice, your privilege to read and take from any poem, any poet, what you want, need, and perhaps find. The essential intimacy is between your own imaginative impulse and what you discover on the page, not "sometime" but in "now" time. Poetry can only be read in the present tense. Does this understanding of an ever-shifting perspective broaden your "seeing"? Your ease with "being seen"?

> ...let [breath] part around your cheeks,
> and then join again, trembling, behind you.

... Even the trees you planted as children
became too heavy long ago; you couldn't carry them.
But the winds ... but the spaces ....

The winds of *our* breath, yours and mine. *Our* spaces. *Ours.*

CHAPTER 4

DISCOVERING YOUR POET'S MIND

Desire the change. O be enthralled with the flame
in which a thing withdraws from you that brims with
    transformations;
that shaping spirit which masters the earthly
loves in the figure's swing nothing as much as the turning
    point.

What closes itself in staying the course is already rigid;
does it think itself secure in the shelter of inconspicuous gray?
Wait, for the hardest warns what is hard from afar.
Woe –: an absent hammer is ready to strike!

Whoever pours themselves forth as a spring the knowing
    knows;
and it leads them with delight through this serene creation
that often ends with beginning and with ending begins.

Every glad space they wander through, marveling,
is a child or grandchild of parting. And the transformed
    Daphne,
since feeling laurel-like, wants you to change yourself into
    wind.

—*The Sonnets to Orpheus* II.12

[*MARK S. BURROWS*]

The practice of paying attention is the heart of what it means to cultivate a "poet's mind." That said, attentiveness constitutes the breadth of a fully human life. According to the French philosopher Simone Weil (1909–1943), a younger contemporary of Rilke's who became one of his ardent readers, this calls us to open ourselves to what is real. It has nothing to do with active concentration but with stillness, with opening ourselves to what *is*, around us and within us. It invites us to be "detached, empty, and ready to be penetrated by the object." It is not a way of grasping the world or managing our lives, but a manner of allowing ourselves to be grasped by it, and, in the process, to be changed by seeing things in new ways. It is the path of resisting being conformed to the world but rather risking the experience of becoming "transformed by the renewing of your mind," as the apostle Paul once put it (Romans 12:2).

This renewal, and not simply the act of writing, is what it means to cultivate your poet's mind. What I recognize in looking back at my own early forays into writing as a young boy is that each poem I had then shaped with painstaking care, written in a clumsy, youthful cursive, was an exercise in the kind of attentiveness that opened me to *experiencing* my life. That capacity more than any other is what changes us from being mere spectators to becoming active participants—in our own life.

But we often fail or refuse to do this, preferring to be achievers or managers of this life, and, in the process, forfeiting our sense of participating in the life-flow that we do not hold, but that holds us. As Rilke put it near the close of the Eighth Elegy,

> And we: spectators, always, everywhere,
> turned toward it all and never looking out!
> Everything overfills us. We put it in order. It falls apart.
> We order it again and fall apart ourselves.

You might also have written poems as a child, or perhaps as a teenager when you were sorting out things that made no sense or seemed to be coming apart in your life. Poems felt, then, like a form suited to give voice to your deep wonderings and longings. With the coming of adulthood, amid all its changing responsibilities, you might have felt yourself increasingly distanced from poetry, discouraged by the time and attention it takes to engage poems given the mounting pressures of your life. Poems, you might have unconsciously surmised, are for poets, and that was not who you were.

This is not to say that you ever relinquished the longing to enter deeply into the soulful depths of your own life or gave up on the reservoir of your inner creativity. Even if it might have seemed far from you at times, you never gave up on that yearning and knew that nothing could ever extinguish that creative potential within you. Despite the swirling changes you were going through, one truth remained clear: a creative life was your sacred birthright. And while you might have had difficulties finding your way back to poetry, that longing never left you. With time, you began to grasp—or be grasped by—what Rilke called the "heartwork" that is a vital part of your life, that *is* your life. This inner work has always been, and remains, the center of your creativity and the source of your passions, all of which inspire the heartbeat of your poet's mind.

Your creativity in all its forms—personal and professional; private and public—has everything to do with your poet's mind. With your ability to engage what Rilke called "the Open," that way of becoming available to the abundance of your life and your place in what Mary Oliver once described as "the family of things." And while there is no map to chart your way into the depths of your soul, the origins of that creativity—which you always carry within you, regardless of circumstances or abilities—is always beckoning despite the pressures that seem to obscure it from view.

To find it, you don't need some kind of magic outside yourself to lead you into the depths of your life. You only need to kindle the yearning that you always carry—and that ultimately carries you. A guide like Rilke might be what you need in looking for signs to lead you back to that path, but you are the only one to discover the treasure of your creative powers and open yourself to realize that, yes, you can begin again. That *you are the future.*

*

What this calls for, above all, finds eloquent expression in the invitation that opens this poem: "Desire the change." Remember that you *are* not what you *were*, or not only this; you are always living in the midst of change, always invited to be attentive to your own becoming. Even this, though, is not something that can be mandated or managed, mirroring as it does something you must discover within yourself. For it is just as true to say that *You are the change you desire.*

Learning to trust your inner compass as you steer your way into the depths of your creativity *is* the beginning of that change. And when you give yourself to doing this, with attentiveness, when you risk opening your life to this path of becoming, you begin to discover what it means to find your poet's mind.

In one of his later *Letters to a Young Poet*, Rilke encouraged young Franz, who by that point had become a ranked military officer, to

> think of the world you carry within yourself, calling this way of thinking anything you wish, whether memories of your childhood or yearning for your future—only be attentive to what arises within you and set it above all else that you observe around you. Your innermost workings are worthy of all you love; this is what you must attend to without losing too much time or giving up your courage to establish your relations to others.

What is the "world" you carry within yourself? It does not require you to become a poet, to live your life as an artist, but it does call you to "live as an artist," as Rick Rubin recently put it in *The Creative Act: A Way of Being,* going on to suggest that

> This is a way of being in the world. A way of perceiving.
> A practice of paying attention. Refining our sensitivity
> to tune in to the more subtle notes. Looking for what
> draws us in and what pushes us away. Noticing what
> feeling tones arise and where they lead.

It is paying attention to "your innermost workings," as Rilke suggests, following a path that steers into the heart's depths where you remember what it means to pay attention. To heed this call is the work of opening yourself to your poet's mind. It is to see your life as a work of art that is *happening*, here and now.

This experience comes not by passively waiting for something magical to happen, not by setting your hopes for a decisive epiphany that might overtake you. It has to do with the work—and it is work—of attending to the depths that cohere in the ordinary moments of "the world you carry within" yourself. It is about embracing the "hereness" of your life, and coming to sense how you belong to "the Whole." For, as Rilke put it in one of his *Sonnets to Orpheus*, "Look, now we must together bear / piecework and parts as if this were the whole (I.16). These are the guides into those creative "ways of perceiving" that lead you to experience deeper belonging and greater connectedness—with yourself, with others, and with this sacred earth that we together indwell.

When this happens, you'll begin to feel how surfaces and depths are joined, how the ordinary stuff of your daily obligations invites you to glimpse the uncharted and unforeseeable depths of your life. Noticing such things leads us step by step into what Rubin calls these "the more subtle notes" in the song that is your life.

On this path of "one-ing," as Rilke sometimes put it, even those apparently irrelevant things in your life can lead you toward a greater sense of wholeness, not somehow beyond but rather squarely—or "roundly"—in the midst of your fears, insecurities, and anxieties. In another of his letters to young Franz, Rilke put it this way:

Allow your judgments their own quiet, undisturbed development, which like every measure of progress must arise from deep within you and can be neither forced nor hurried. Everything is about bearing this to the point of giving birth. To live as an artist, in your understanding and in your creative life, depends on letting each impression and each seed of a feeling come to completion, entirely in itself, in the dark, in the unsayable, in the unconscious, beyond the reach of one's own understanding, and with deep humility and patience to wait for the hour when a new clarity is born.

This advice offers a profound measure of insight into what creativity means. Ours is the work of "giving birth" to the creative life we carry within us. Not that this is an easy thing to do. That insight calls to us "beyond the reach of our own understanding," to those unconscious depths which hold what we gradually come to know as our creativity, which is ultimately "unsayable."

An effective way to be true to this source is to open ourselves to its wisdom. To *re-mind* ourselves of this over and over in our lives. That openness invites us to discover that this wisdom is not something lying outside of us but within, for it is there, in the heart's innermost depths, that we begin to learn what it means to cultivate our poet's mind. It is in this manner that we remember that Rilke's call—and mine—to "live as an artist" beckons us to open ourselves to what we carry deep within, "in the dark, in the unsayable, in the unconscious, beyond the reach of [our] understanding."

This is a difficult task in cultures like ours that prize measurable achievements, effective strategies, ascertainable results. All of which turns us from living the questions, enervating the poet's mind we all always carry within ourselves.

*

The source of your deepest creativity has to do not with "grasping" your life but rather with learning to embrace it for what it is, and for what it is becoming—which is to see and be transformed in that seeing. As Rilke put it in his novel, *The Notebooks of Malte Laurids Brigge,*

> I don't know where this comes from, but I find that everything is now touching me more deeply than before, no longer staying at the place where it once came to an end. I have an innerness that I previously did not know about. Everything now goes to that depth.

And he goes on to add—and this is a crucial part of cultivating your poet's mind: "And I don't really understand what happens there."

What Rilke is alluding to, this *re-minding*, has little to do with technique and everything to do with opening yourself to what he simply calls your "innerness." It points to your capacity to see your life, with its surfaces and depths, in relation to the "outer" world where you dwell, to begin from within before turning to what surrounds you. Failing to do this is a sure way to stifle your creativity, which has little to do with something outside of you. It is a way of "ripening," another word Rilke favored. It is a way of opening to your inner life where you might begin to see how everything in your life, both surfaces and depths alike—"each impression and seed of a feeling"—moves from birthing into "becoming." All of which is to say that the creativity that is the heart of your poet's mind has little to do with writing poetry. At least not in a literal sense.

Your discovery of that mind, within yourself, has to do with the more essential work by which you find yourself learning to pay attention to your life, and to see that "that shaping spirit, which masters the earthly / loves in the figure's swing nothing as much as the turning point." The urgings you find at the "turning points" in your life, when you find yourself "enthralled with the flame / in which a thing withdraws from you that brims with transformations," are vital to your poet's mind.

In fact, I would suggest that these deep, natural inner urges *are* that mind. They are not waiting to be discovered outside—in a workshop on self-expression or in a program in creative writing—but within, announcing themselves sometimes in a quiet whisper and at other times with a raucous roar.

Howsoever they come, they invite you to say "yes!" to life, to risk living authentically and courageously from your heart. They call you to take what you have been given and embrace not who you have been, but who you are becoming. They await your making something of this life, regardless of what others say or feel about you. This is the calling that invites you to give your life a shape that sings, to embody Rilke's conviction that "song is being"—and "being is song." To begin to respond to this invitation is to answer Rilke's bold call to "desire the change!" and to realize that "the designing spirit which masters the earthly / loves in the figure's swing nothing as much as the turning point."

Whatever your poet's mind might invite you to become, in whatever forms you envision or experience your creativity, it has everything to do with embracing—and, yes, loving—those "turning points" in your life, for it is these that remind you that you are never finished growing, that you are always on the journey of *becoming*. And here is the crucial point that grounds all this: opening yourself to your poet's mind does not simply invite you to change. No, this mind *is* that change. As a birthing, it invites you to call upon your capacity to create from deep within yourself, first of all, to make something of your own life, which is the deepest and truest and most urgently important business of being human. Of being *yourself*. When you trust in the resource of your creativity, you become ever more alive to who you are—and more to the point, who you are *becoming*. For *you are the future*. This is what grounds you, opening you to live in the forward flow of things through the power of your own creativity. This is what it means to begin to discover your poet's mind. The rest will follow.

*

What does it mean to heed the call to find your poet's mind? This has to do with something at once deep, essential, and accessible in your life: it is the path by which you root your life in the dynamic energies of your becoming. It is a path that leads into your inner creativity, inviting you to indwell what Rilke called "the Open" in your life—which is to say, to give yourself to an expansive, spacious way of being, one by which you refuse the false lure of being reduced to what is safe. This path calls you to open yourself to engaging the abundance of your life, untamed and wild as it might be. As a wise writer recently put it, each of us is capable of saying of ourselves, "I am the poet of the poem that is my life."

Of course, much in our culture argues against this. We find ourselves saturated with images of what "success" looks like with all its external glitter and outward forms of achievement. Already at an early age we find ourselves bombarded with examples of how we should look, act, and feel, shaming us for our inadequacies. We are even tempted to set aside the deep, inner drive of creativity to reduce our lives to outward ambition, giving over our inner freedom to satisfy others' expectations. Nothing good can come of this. Yet we accommodate ourselves in ways that diminish our sense of self and blunt our creativity.

What, then, does it mean to become a poet of "the poem that is your life"? Rilke responded to this with what he voiced as an invitation: *You must change your life.* You must learn to indwell the "becomingness" of your own life. And you must discover how this connects with the lives of others, shaped as this is by what you cannot yet know but released from what you—or others—thought you must be.

Vincent Van Gogh knew this already as a young artist, insisting in an early letter to his brother that the life of an artist depended upon "continuous work, but also not giving up your opinion at the bidding of such and such a person." He went on to say that just as "art demands persistent work, work in spite of everything," it also calls for "a continuous observation." A life shaped by attentiveness and energized by an engaged and creative way of opening to the world, which often enough invites us to venture forth on unfamiliar paths, which is rarely easy work.

In describing a life shaped by the inner urgings of "a continuous observation," Rilke turned to the metaphor of fire. He knew that a poet's mind calls us to engage "the flame" we carry within us. It points to the passion by which you come to see that even "what's taken from you brims with transformations."

This is a crucial insight: to remember that even your losses and disappointments hold within them the invitation to change. This is the mind by which you come to embrace your life as more than you can imagine, immersed as it is in your own becoming. A life guided by the "shaping spirit" of creativity that "loves ... the turning point," that invites you to let go of the familiar even when this might require that you drop something you are good at and others prize—if holding onto it prevents you from beginning anew with your own life.

The central question each of us faces is whether we can open ourselves to see this as the path that invites us to face the unknown with curiosity and compassion. To affirm that, yes, *we are the future*. To recognize the presence of this becoming is a crucial first step in entrusting our lives to "the Open," which is how we begin to make room within us for our poet's mind. The alternative is a stark one, as Rilke goes on to say: "What closes itself in staying *is* already the hardened" (II.12).

In the memoir that Lou Andreas-Salomé published two years after Rilke's death, she wrote of the danger of "binding" oneself to precisely this: what is "hardened" by being accepted, safe, or familiar. Such choices, she knew, dampen our creativity and, in the worst case, render our lives inert.

In describing various conventional attitudes by which we might be tempted to see creativity as something external to ourselves, she reminds us—following Rilke's lead—that our inner life, the creative power of our soul, calls for "flow." She portrays this path as one she discovered over the decades of her intimate friendship with Rilke:

> To be sure, there is another attitude toward art. . . . One
> finds it lying behind every form of art and the complex,
> expressive forms of the imagination: each one of us

leads an imaginative existence, from the most elemen-
tal to the most sophisticated levels of our experience,
from our most alert thoughts to our deepest dreams
that come to us in the nights. And the more distanced
we are from our controlling consciousness, and the
more immersed we are in what comes to us from the
soul's depths, the more we are able to draw on, the more
convinced we are of the poet within us, indeed *the poet
within every person.*

To look at this from another angle, you might think of your poet's mind
as leading you *to experience the world around you as . . . becoming.* To see
the creativity of your life in those "turning points" which open to what
you cannot yet see, inviting you to stretch beyond the bounds of conven-
tional thinking—your own, of course, but also that of others.

Another way to envision this, as Rilke does in this poem, is to see this
creativity as gesturing toward an uncontainable abundance: "Whoever
pours out as a spring the knowing knows," an experience that "leads him
[or her] delighted through this bright creation / that often ends with
beginning and with ending begins." Turning points often beckon us to
live boldly; they can open us to face our losses with the creative determi-
nation to begin again. And again.

As the poem unfolds, Rilke gives voice to a warning, reminding us
that the path of creativity, the call of "the poet's mind," cannot remove
from us the barriers and challenges that often thwart our creativity. As
he puts it in the lines that follow:

> Wait, for the hardest warns what is hard from afar.
> Woe–: an absent hammer is ready to strike

What is Rilke pointing to with this strange metaphor of an "absent ham-
mer"? Your doubts, perhaps, and surely your shame and anxiety. Maybe
even your shattered sense of self. All of these pressures that "harden" you
can dissuade you from opening your heart to your own creativity. To

your becoming. And they will just as surely discourage you from availing yourself of your poet's mind.

Such difficulties are inevitable, but they are never final. Rilke reminds us of this as the poem unfolds, and we do well to bear this in mind—to keep hold of it when we face with fear such "absent hammers." For when such challenges come, when setbacks beset us as they will, we must remember to give ourselves again and again to "the shaping spirit" we carry within us. Only in this way might we begin to discover that

> Every glad space they wander through, marveling,
>   is a child or grandchild of parting.

That is, this creativity often comes to us as a hard-won gain, after the often persistent and debilitating experience over "generations" of part- ing in our life. Rilke knew this himself through the devastating depres- sion he faced during World War I and through the years that followed when he found himself unable to find the source of inspiration that he so longed for in order to complete the long-interrupted *Duino Elegies*.

We do well to remember that when the well runs dry, when our muse remains silent, when we feel ourselves succumbing to discourage- ment, we may learn to trust those very silences, knowing that such "glad spaces" will come. And, when they do, they invite us to "wander through [them] in amazement" again. And again.

*

Rilke closes this sonnet with a reference to the mythological fig- ure, Daphne. It invokes a story Rilke knew from reading Ovid's *Metamorphoses* in which this beautiful young nymph found herself pur- sued by Apollo who was overcome with desire. In the moment when she sensed her capture was near, she prayed that she might be "transformed into a laurel tree" to escape. With that fraught moment in mind the poet invites us to realize that we, too, have the capacity to be changed, not into a laurel but into "wind." This is the gift of "the shaping spirit" that opens us to the flow of change. This reminds us that we are most truly ourselves not in our *being* but in our *becoming*.

"Desire the change": the guiding voice we have found in Rilke and shared with you over the course of this book is magnified in this remarkable opening. If you could come to live by heeding this invitation—from day to day, season to season, and year to year—you will begin to discover your poet's mind, and that is what matters most. You might find yourself unburdened, a little, of your fear of losing who you thought you were, discovering yourself as one who is in the process of becoming. Whatever else a poet is, she is a "maker" who takes what life brings, with all its highs and lows, and finds in it the creative powers that refuse to be silenced, that resist premature defeat.

Whether or not you ever dare to write a single line or heed Rilke's invitation to "dance the orange," the call to "desire the change" is the heart of the matter. It is the grounding energy of your life. As the painter Robert Henri once put it, "the object isn't to make art, it's to be in that wonderful state that makes art inevitable." Inevitable, not simply possible. How do you find your way into that "wonderful state" in your life? How do you open yourself to discovering what it means to awake, little by little, to your poet's mind? To see your life itself as a work of art? As you find the path that leads you into that discovery, what will you do with this inevitability? How will you make a "poem" of your life?

*

As we wrote this book, each of us felt guided by the ways Rilke has been both an encouraging and a challenging voice, one that has continuously invited our creative response and engendered a poignant resonance within our lives. It is our hope that your journey with us has opened you to discovering your own "poet's mind," one that calls you to open yourself to what *is* while also daring to "desire the change" in your life. Rilke's example reminds us that when we give the judgment about our own creativity to others, we rarely find our poet's mind and often succumb to the inner shadows of self-criticism and doubt.

When this happens, we forfeit something essential about ourselves: namely, the capacity to see that dimension of our lives—our essential and inviolable creativity—not as something we should entrust to others to manage for us. And surely this reminds us not to allow others' judgments to prevent us from claiming as our own "the shaping spirit" we carry within ourselves, that creative power which "masters the earthly" and "loves in the figure's swing nothing as much as the turning point."

This "wiser way" is always one you must discover *for yourself*, and *in yourself*, and doing so is the work that opens to you the character of your poet's mind: *You are the future*. I would even say that this is as inviolable a part of your creative life as breathing is for your body. The one question you need to ask is about what you are doing with the essential seedbed of your creativity. Which no one other than you can reach, even if they might well encourage—or discourage—you in your desire to find it. As you begin to open yourself to its powers, give it room—as the shape of your truest self—to create within you. And, yes: to create *you*, again and again, through the imaginative power of your poet's mind.

This might even lead you to take up Rilke's call to "dance the orange," in whatever shape that might take. You don't have to know all the movements to do this; just step out and begin. As you do, the dance itself will lead you.

CHAPTER 5

WHO AM I?

O the losses into the All, Marina, the stars that are falling!
We do not become "more" wherever we fling ourselves,
    to whichever star! In the whole, all things are already
    numbered.
So, when anyone falls, the perfect sum is not lessened.
Whoever lets go in their fall, dives into the source and is
    healed.
Would it all be a game? A changing of names? A waiting?
And no greater sense yet gained of home?

Waves, Marina, we are ocean! Depths, Marina, we are sky!
Earth, Marina, we are earth! Spring a thousand times over.
Like larks made invisible by their bursting songs,
we start out with jubilations greater than ourselves,
until burdens bring our song down, down into a lament.
…Minor gods also want to be praised…
…Nothing belongs to us…

—an untitled poem from a letter of 1925

[*STEPHANIE DOWRICK*]

These magnificent lines sing to me like a hymn to existence. Perhaps they were received that way by the exiled younger Russian poet and activist, Marina Tsvetaeva, who, for a brief period, was engaged in an epistolary romance with Rilke that seems to have stirred and inspired him also. I cannot tire of reading them and re-filling myself with their symphonic exuberance. How powerfully they remind me that we live in a world of wonder. And that even if my part in that world is very small, that I must not think myself "small."

> Waves, Marina, we are ocean! Depths, Marina, we are sky!
> Earth, Marina, we are earth! Spring a thousand times over.

Every moment as we lift our eyes to see, to truly see, nature presents herself to us in her manifold glory and sometimes terrifying power. With no effort or special claim, I am part of something utterly wonder-filled. So was Marina, despite the horrendously difficult times she lived in. So are you. So is each of us. This is where we transcend all the loaded, binary, diminishing judgments that would divide us from one another.

Who am I *in essence*? Who are *you* in essence? "You are gods, all of you. Children of the Most High," sings the Psalmist in the Book of Psalms (Psalm 82). Are we the "minor gods" Rilke sings of in the poem above? Perhaps we are. Yet Rilke goes on to say, "Nothing belongs to us." At least not permanently. While we live, though, *we* belong to everything. *Everything.* And, most essentially, we belong to life itself. Life is our gift. Consciousness is our gift. Awareness of and perhaps identifying with soul, spirit, oneness, wholeness: our gift. None of us left out.

One of the psychological masters from whom I have learned much about the human condition is Roberto Assagioli, a noted neurologist and psychiatrist and founder of a spiritually informed psychology called psychosynthesis. As an Italian Jew, the years of the Second World War must have been terrifying to him. His losses were immense. Among his "international crimes"—according to the Fascist rule of the day—was "praying for peace and inviting others to join him." His tragedies were intimately personal as he lost his only son, in his twenties, who died of lung disease resulting from the deprivations of war. Yet, in contemplating the infinite brilliance of the night sky over a darkened Rome, Assagioli knew himself not as an insignificant "nobody" or as a hated and despised Jew, but as someone intrinsically part of a wondrous universe. Could any perspective be more exquisite?

Love, wisdom, and creativity are values or expressions of our humanity that Assagioli believed Freud left out of his schema, at considerable cost. The "synthesis" in psychosynthesis speaks to a regaining of wholeness, just as Rilke does so powerfully and prominently in his most transporting work, and in the face of his own very real psychological and existential challenges. *Love. Wisdom. Creativity.*

*

Poetry, like all the expressive arts, demonstrates that we are a species capable of awe, magnificence, and praise. And of unlimited vision in how we regard this most fundamental of all questions: *Who am I?* Seeking meaning is a primary task of consciousness. How, though, do we grasp that?

How do we take that drive for meaning into ourselves as Assagioli did—and hold ourselves steady from the inside out even when others may view us through the eyes of indifference, or contempt? Or if we are seen not as a complex, striving human being but in reductive stereotypical terms by those who believe they have a "natural" or even "God-given" right to judge us? How do we remain grounded in the great humane values of decency, integrity, and care for others when it's those qualities that are absent in much of what passes for public leadership? Or when we take our sense of "who I am" solely from the outside, and not from our matchless inner knowledge of an ever-unfolding self?

What we identify *with* is critical to our sense of identity. It is no secret that most of us live in fast-moving societies where superficial values distract us, banal judgments are normalized, and divisiveness and hyper-competitiveness are instilled even in our youngest children based on factors over which they have no control.

In this atmosphere, status and material wealth—however ugly their origins—may count for more than character. Or kindness. The hyper-wealthy are judged by separate standards from those impoverished by economic systems set to entrap them. In the earliest years of school, children learn the vocabulary of insufficiency and are warned: few can be "winners." They learn, as we do, that individual "excellence" supposedly beats community-building virtues of cooperation, collaboration, and inclusion. They also discover that "losers" are blamed for their own fate. "What do you want to be when you grow up?" is a question that seldom refers to anything beyond an occupation or profession. Who one *is*, what values one lives by, is rarely part of that enquiring conversation.

Yet you *already are* yourself in essence: an expression of life's infinite variety, the embodiment of soul, both like and unlike any other. In fact, however others seek to pigeon-hole you, *you are more than that*. More than your nationality, gender, abilities, disabilities, triumphs, failures, virtues—more than body, feelings, mind, instincts. You *have* a body, feelings, mind, instincts; you are *more than* those. You are also more than whatever roles your life has led you toward, or you have chosen. *You are the future.*

"All the world's a stage," wrote William Shakespeare, "and all the men and women merely players. They have their exits and their entrances and each man in his time plays many parts...." *Roles, yes, but is that my real self? Is that who I am?*

> In the whole, all things are already numbered.
> So, when anyone falls, the perfect sum is not lessened.
> Whoever lets go in their fall, dives into the source and is
>   healed.
> Would it all be a game? A changing of names? A waiting?
> And no greater sense yet gained of home?

*

Who am I? is a question that others will rush to answer for you. Nationalism rears up here, with quite a surprising number of nations bestowing on their citizens the uncritical expectation that their nationality is "the greatest in the world." By declaring himself "European,"

Rilke defied this absurdity. So did Virginia Woolf when she wrote: "As a woman I have no country. As a woman my country is the whole world."

Institutional religions keenly offer ready-made definitions, some of which extend beyond this life and into eternity. It's true that in an age of confusion and widespread loneliness, the urge to belong, even to be quite narrowly defined as the price of belonging, is understandable. Extreme political groups certainly offer this, and sometimes groups that may not see themselves as "extreme" yet are overtly exclusive, defined by their differences from those with whom they vigorously disagree. Religious groups across all faiths can and do offer community, care, a sense of meaning, and sometimes a respite from self-inquiry that can feel like a relief. Yet religious groups particularly, if anchored to rigid, patriarchal forms, are notorious for their distrust of deeply contemplated *Who am I* questions. Almost invariably, they want to tell you exactly who you are. And predict your fate.

Those are gang rules and just as deadly.

When it comes to race, gender, and sexuality, religious communities often have the most obvious hierarchies of inclusion and exclusion, of identity and belonging. But again, such hierarchies are not limited to religious communities. They pass for normal in many nations, including Australia and the United States. The First Nations of Australia—the oldest surviving cultures in our world—were "given" the opportunity to vote in 1962, though it was not until 1984 that they were compelled to vote as everyone else of voting age was and is in this country. In 2023, First Nations asked via a national referendum to be recognized in the Australian Constitution and to have their own Voice to the Federal Parliament. Their decades-long efforts were supported by the Australian Labor government but rejected by the conservative opposition and a majority of voters in yet another act of dispossession.

In 1963, the magnificent African American writer James Baldwin— one of the 20th century's most influential intellectuals—wrote:

> You were born where you were born and faced the
> future that you faced because you were Black and for no

other reason. The limits of your ambition were, thus, expected to be set forever. You were born into a society which spelled out with brutal clarity, and in as many ways as possible, that you were a worthless human being. You were not expected to aspire to excellence: you were expected to make peace with mediocrity.

Examples of economic injustice are everywhere. So are the media fables that entrench or excuse them. Favored myths of "hard work" and the rewards presumed to come with it need vigorous exposing. These myths suggest that those who do not "make it" fail to do so because—again—of *personal* insufficiencies: *Whoever I am, I am not enough*. The sky-high structural barriers that allow privilege to assert its own mediocrity are rendered invisible, except to those who daily suffer from them.

Even the relative few among minorities who do "make it" on the majority's terms are reminded in small and large ways that their belonging is conditional. They are used as examples to others: "See, she/he/they made it…so why couldn't you?" The worst of these dehumanizing tropes are reserved for a hierarchy based on skin color. This abjectly disrupts the natural relatedness between peoples and the planet on which our safety and well-being so conspicuously depend. Those messages go deep, though, and can also divide us from a self-trusting sense of ourselves. *Who am I?*

Despite this—and maybe in healthy rebellion against it—the timeless virtues flourish. Kindness is real in millions of lives, along with courage, consideration, a capacity to forgive and work for peace, a reluctance to cause or support harm, a belief in humankind's fundamental goodness and our capacity to get along. In such cases, the question *Who am I?* includes within it the larger one, *Who are we?* Who are we as a single, interrelated, vast, and diverse human family, with an appetite and need for meaning unique to our species?

*

Viktor Frankl is a writer I have read and re-read with profound grat-
itude since my mid-teens. For me, he is a primary teacher of what life
might be when we can allow ourselves to feel appreciation for life itself,
and not just for what we can "do" with it. A psychiatrist, philosopher,
founder of logotherapy, and concentration camp survivor, Frankl helps
us to understand that one of the worst "poverties" is a meaningless exis-
tence. Or one in which your greatest excitement is pursuing an entirely
material goal or following—living through—the successes or failures of
something or someone extraneous to yourself. In other words, living a
life that expresses little of who *you are* or are becoming, except as a spec-
tator or consumer. "Reality shows" are an extreme but common example
of how tenuous our links to "reality" will be when we are seduced into
emotional responses to confected dramas that distract us from the very
real drama of living in divisive, insecure environments where peace of
mind—as well as meaning—can be difficult to locate.

In his famed book, *Man's Search for Meaning*, Frankl wrote that "life
is not primarily a quest for pleasure, as Sigmund Freud believed, nor a
quest for power, as Alfred Adler taught, but a quest for meaning. The
greatest task for any person is to find meaning in his or her life."

Finding meaning co-exists with finding a sense of self that is at least
somewhat independent of others' formulaic expectations—yet is also
alert to the effects of your attitudes and choices on others. Uniquely
individual, yes you are, *and you are also* one among billions living into the
truths of interdependence.

> Whoever lets go in their fall, dives into the source and is
>   healed.
> Would it all be a game? A changing of names? A waiting?
> *And no greater sense yet gained of home* [my italics].

It is a stronger sense of inner reality, too, and the patience as well as
wisdom that can come from knowledge of our own gifts of inward-
ness, that will best help us survive the harsh vicissitudes that befall so

many. Marie-Louise von Franz, an early associate of Carl Jung—and a gifted translator of texts for him, from Greek, Latin, and Arabic into German—called this inner reality, "a sense of solid ground within." If this "solid ground" metaphor resonates with you, it gives rise to a sense of steadiness and integrity that can be affected by others but is not determined by them.

Meaning is *always* about relatedness, *always* about caring beyond one's own garden gate, *always* about seeking the nourishment of creating good and diminishing any impulses toward harm. It is always also, though, about regarding one's own self with respect. This necessarily includes valuing your own efforts, even and especially in the hardest, darkest times. "...when anyone falls, the perfect sum is not lessened..." *The perfect sum is not lessened.*

Von Franz herself warned against disowning your own integrity and projecting idealized forms onto others:

> Following your own star means...having to find out a completely new way for yourself instead of just going on the trodden path everybody else runs along. That's why there's always been a tendency in humans to project the uniqueness and the greatness of their own inner self onto outer personalities and become the servants, the devoted servants, admirers, and imitators of outer personalities. It is much easier to admire a great personality and become a pupil or follower of a guru or a religious prophet, or an admirer of a big, official personality—a President of the United States—or live your life for some military general whom you admire. That is much easier than following your own star.

Discovering your own truths, holding onto trust in your own goodness and that of others—despite the daily horrors we witness on the news and perhaps in our own neighborhood or home—has become a near-defiant and surely redeeming option.

How exhilarating that poetry can tease this out so effectively.

Reading Rilke frees the non-linear mind. It demands a cerebral foxtrot. It carries you home to your natural creativity. That is itself a psychological release. You can so readily be crushed by those who may never contemplate "us" as "ocean," "earth," "sky"—"Spring a thousand times over"—created for joy, exuberance, the choosing of *life*. Yet. Yet. "They"—those who have lost touch with their power to exult— are also as much of part of us as any other.

This is the essential spiritual law of *interbeing*, and this poem is soaked in it. Only an unconditional valuing of all life, of human life no matter our nationality, sexuality or gender, race or ethnicity, keeps us safe. Only such valuing secures our own dignity, as well as that of others. This defies the misery of binary thinking. Or the delusion that the only lives that matter are those most like our own. Our highest responsibility is to live with meaningful care for others. And for our beloved shared planet. For "all creatures great and small." *And for ourselves. Your life is as worthy of honoring as any other.*

The poem above sings that. It gives me pause—and quiet joy—that it may be poetry that shows we cannot consider *Who am I?* without also asking *Who are we?* For, surely, we cannot consider social change without a re-visioning and re-valuing of beauty, art, life, and truth? Of love, wisdom, and creativity? Of kindness and delight? Of forgiveness, not of the big things only but also our everyday misapprehensions, or idiocies?

It was an American woman, the suffrage activist Helen Todd, who called for "bread for all, and roses too." It is Rilke, though, who writes in what were to become the last months of his life:

> Waves, Marina, we are ocean! Depths, Marina, we are sky!
> Earth, Marina, we are earth! Spring a thousand times over.
> Like larks made invisible by their bursting songs,
> we start out with jubilations greater than ourselves,
> until burdens bring our song down, down into a lament.
> …Minor gods also want to be praised…
> …Nothing belongs to us…

Nothing belongs to us, at least not for long.

That makes all the grasping for more than we could need in a hundred lifetimes even more absurd. It is through our *being*, presence, and sensibility that we leave traces, an imprint, however humble our outer lives. "Who says that all must vanish"? asked Rilke in the first line of another poem. Communal societies see the hyper-individualism of our own as an aberration that is inevitably destructive of individual contentment, ironically, as well as of common good.

Communal societies hold relationships to people, species, and planet earth as primary. *They know that individuals thrive who naturally look out for one another—and feel others' care and interest in return.* We are undeniably part of a greater whole. Undeniably. During the Covid years, a willingness to prioritize keeping others safe saved millions of lives. Perhaps hundreds of millions of lives. It makes a striking contrast to those asserting their right to abandon public health precautions in the name of individual freedom, even when that meant risking infecting others—including exhausted health workers—or dying themselves. Listen again to Rilke, no "believer" in any conventional sense, but a true poet:

> O the losses into the All, Marina, the stars that are falling!
> We do not become "more" wherever we fling ourselves,
>   to whichever star! In the whole, all things *are* already
>   numbered.
> So, when anyone falls, the perfect sum is not lessened.

Yet, if we could glimpse ourselves transcending even the most compelling "identities" and consider that we may be spiritual beings on a human journey, perhaps our differences of culture, physical form, desires, skin color, or gender could be a matter of celebration. We could circle back to Hermann Hesse's words: "The mind is international and supra-national. It ought to serve not war and annihilation, but peace and reconciliation." Peace and reconciliation even within ourselves.

Who am I? again yields to the more inclusive *Who are we?* Or even, *What are we capable of being?*

> Would it all be a game? A changing of names? A waiting?
> And no greater sense yet gained of home?
> Waves, Marina, we are ocean! Depths, Marina, we are sky!
> Earth, Marina, we are earth! Spring a thousand times over.

*

My own life as a seeker and writer has been further inspired by the words of George Fox, a founding 17th-century Quaker, who coined the phrase: "Walk cheerfully over this earth, answering that of God in everyone." *Everyone*, without exception. Because, in that logic, either there is "that of God" in everyone, or in no one.

Is this proclamation of the equal dignity of all lives difficult to comprehend? Is it hard to live? Quakers certainly do strive to live it, at least those who follow the Peace Testimony that begins: "*We utterly deny all outward wars and strife, and fighting with outward weapons, for any end, or under any pretence whatever; this is our testimony to the whole world…*" Jains—of whom there are about six million—take this further. Their commitment to non-violence ("ahismā") is such that they take care not to kill any living beings, however tiny, nor to commit acts of violence in thought or word.

That last principle of non-violence truly challenges me. Perhaps you also? When I write on or simply contemplate the gross political and social injustices we see everywhere, I am not calm. Nor am I calm when it comes to those with crazy power to harm. *How dare they…? How could they…?* It is returning to that unconditionally inclusive *everyone*—"that of God in everyone" that eventually steadies me. And lets me know that my part, however small, counts too. Ocean. Sky. Earth. *Spring a thousand times.*

In his Seventh Elegy, Rilke—far from an optimist and turned away from any orthodoxy—pulls us back from too much fixation on outer events as the sole evidence of evolution in our slow-learning species. His lines in that Elegy include these:

> Nowhere, beloved, does any
> world exist except within.
> Life spends itself in
> the act of transformation,
> dissolving, bit by bit,
> the world as it appeared.

Nowhere, beloved. Rilke, the supreme poet of the inner spaces: guide, not guru. And while there's no hiding here from outer events and their effects, his "permission" is clear: take your sense of Who am I? from the inside, from your glimpses of soul, from your "ground within." Each of us, "however lonely," is already and always "someone." Each of us is already and always part of that greater whole. Each of us has conscious choices to make that will also "make" us. It is encouraging then that in this same, sometimes mystifying Elegy, Rilke also states: "To be here at all is a glory." Indeed, yes. That insight alone sings to me of healing. And salvation.

*

In 1926, during part of what was to be the final year of his life, Rilke— just into his fifties—was writing to Marina Tsvetaeva, in her early thirties, already a mother of three and a renowned poet. These letters began as a three-way sharing between the two poets and writer Boris Pasternak. At Pasternak's urging, Rilke sent her his newly published *The Sonnets to Orpheus* and *Duino Elegies*; she responded with the highest possible praise of the poet: "You are the very incarnation of poetry."

All three were enduring desolation with loss of country, belonging—and hope, both personal and political. The two Russians had lived through the Revolution of 1917 and the famine that followed. Tsvetaeva also had to bear the horrifying death of one of her two daughters who died of starvation in 1920 after she had placed both the girls in a state orphanage, believing that would keep them safe. Indeed, neither she nor her family would ever know any degree of safety, or peace, which certainly intensifies the poignancy of this poem.

Yet, in returning to the theme of writing, we can more easily imagine those sublime letters as both a comfort and further pain for Tsvetaeva, particularly when she discovered that Rilke's feelings for her as a woman would be strictly confined to the safety of letter writing. Tsvetaeva was, as so many women in his orbit had been before her, a desired and desiring person. Nonetheless, the distances between them were set by Rilke. *Who was she to him?* That must have been a question Marina asked of herself. We can only guess at her answer. As we must so often guess at the answer when we too wonder: *Who am I to you? Who am I, to my own self? Who are you to me?*

Rilke was writing to Tsvetaeva from the Valais in Switzerland, a place he described as "not only among the loveliest of landscapes I have ever seen, but also, to an exceptional extent, offering manifold reflections of our own inner world." It is a place of mountains, valleys, and dramatic seasonal changes, where the reflections of high peaks were often seen doubled in quiet lake water. It is a place where Rilke found "a warm (though not yet warmed for good, unfortunately) wall," and wrote his words to Tsvetaeva, "riveting the lizards in their tracks by intoning it":

> O the losses into the All, Marina, the stars that are falling!
> We do not become "more" wherever we fling ourselves,
>   to whichever star! In the whole, all things are already
>   numbered.
> So, when anyone falls, the perfect sum is not lessened.
> Whoever lets go in their fall, dives into the source and is
>   healed.
> Would it all be a game? A changing of names? A waiting?
> And no greater sense yet gained of home?
> Waves, Marina, we are ocean! Depths, Marina, we are sky!
> Earth, Marina, we are earth! Spring a thousand times over.

Like larks made invisible by their bursting songs,
we start out with jubilations greater than ourselves,
until burdens bring our song down, down into a lament.
…Minor gods also want to be praised…
…Nothing belongs to us…

How does the *Who am I?* question sit with this confidence that *Nothing belongs to us?* And how does it accord with the claim that "we do not become 'more' / wherever we fling ourselves, to whichever / star!"? How does our *becoming* fit with "In the whole, all things are already numbered"?

I treasure the poet's confidence: "when anyone falls, the perfect sum is not lessened." A beginning that has no beginning, an "ending" that is not final. It is wholeness and perhaps something like the Buddhist concept of *sunyata*—sometimes translated as emptiness, also "openness" or even "thusness." In moments of deep meditation, when the organizing mind slows, you might glimpse this "no-thought." Surrender happens. Presence happens. A subduing of tension may happen.

Perhaps I seek the solace that Rilke himself wished *not* to provide. Nonetheless, I find solace here. Rilke is surely saying, *whoever you are*, don't sell yourself short. Don't pretend insignificance. You have no need to bargain, cajole, plead. You need never beg to belong or to be worthy. You *do* belong. You *are* worthy. Don't fall either for the carnival songs of a material universe. Your belonging is to something far greater. Magnificent. Timeless. Infinite. *You are the future.*

Rilke speaks frankly to say, you, we, are capable of jubilation "*greater than ourselves.*" Ecstasy is your original song. Yes, you can be reduced by sorrow to a lament, or to silence. You will be brought down. You will fall out of touch with wholeness. Perhaps briefly, agonizingly, out of love with life itself. Burdens were what Rilke knew intimately. But, in this place and poem of remembering, let's recall what liberation is. *Nothing belongs to me.* Yet, I belong to the Whole. As do you.

It was within months of his dying that Rilke wrote in this way to Marina, mindful of what she had already lost. As we one day will leave this earth, this body, nothing any longer will "belong" to us. Nor will we "belong" any longer to the earth. All those coveted things we call "belongings" will cease to be—for us. Rilke was speaking to himself.

Did he want also to encourage Marina in the grievous existential pain she was barely enduring—which included persecution, loss of her homeland, and the torture and death of loved ones, a burden so great that she finally succumbed to it in suicide? He knew well the diminishment of spirit accompanying physical and grave emotional suffering. In his place of suffering, he met Marina fully and lifted her—and us—beyond it.

> …when anyone falls, the perfect sum is not lessened.
> Whoever lets go in their fall, dives into the source and is
>   healed….

CHAPTER 6

MORE THAN YOUR MISTAKES

We knew nothing of his amazing head
in which his eyes ripened like apples. But
his body still glows like a streetlamp
in which his gaze, now extinguished,

continues and shines. Otherwise, his curving
chest couldn't have blinded you, and the quiet twist
of his loins wouldn't have brought a smile
to the groin where his begetting lay.

Otherwise, this stone would've been marred,
there where the shoulders seem to fall,
and wouldn't shimmer like a predator's hide,

couldn't have burst forth from all its edges like
an exploding star—because here there is no place
that doesn't see you. You must change your life.

—"Archaic Torso of Apollo"

[*MARK S. BURROWS*]

Of the many memorable lines in Rilke's poems, few are as well-known—
and under-practiced—as this one: *"You must change your life."* Most

among us realize the truth of this claim when we come face to face with dead ends in our own lives. When things fall apart. When we run head-on into the storms of our own confused mistakes or find ourselves towed into others' blunders or betrayals. And yet we are stubbornly reluctant to turn; unwilling to concede that we might have failed; unable or unwilling to change.

I've heard this voice barking away in the back of my own mind a thousand times, and still I cling to the familiar, refusing to change even when things aren't working well. Or at all. I know I'm not alone in this. But how do we change, especially when doing so requires that we give up our security, relinquish our certainties, admit our mistakes? What courage does this take?

As I ponder Rilke's call, I also wonder about his intent.

On the surface, the claim stands as a command: *"You must change... your life."* But it might well be that he intended something quite different with it. What happens if we open ourselves to hearing it as an invitation? Not as a call of duty, but rather as an invitation that opens us to imagine, first of all, that we *could* change—and, finally, *must*—if we would be true to ourselves? This is something altogether different. And, strangely, both unsettling and reassuring at once.

To see this, though, calls for a grasp of the whole poem which is far less familiar than this final claim. And to be honest, it's a difficult one to sort out. Rilke wrote the poem after visiting the Louvre in Paris where he found himself standing, in the Gallery of Antiquity, before a dismembered body of the ancient god Apollo. Gone are his legs and arms. Even his head is missing. What is left is a partial, worn-down torso. This figure has had a hard go of it, and in this he is not unlike the rest of us as we steer our way through the inevitable losses of life.

What's startling about the image here is Rilke's sense of what is still vibrant and alive in this hobbled torso, and how he conveys this to us. This broken-down Apollo is still brimming with energy: "his body still glows like a streetlamp." The gaze of his now absent eyes still "shines" as we gaze upon them, if only in our imagining. What we know to be absent—the god's arms and legs and even his head—points not to what is *gone*, or not only to this, but to what somehow still *is*. As is true in my life and yours amid the scars we bear and the losses we have endured.

The problem is that we don't face loss well in our "have-it-all-now" culture. We too often hide our pain from others or turn from it ourselves. And, given the magnitude of suffering around us, we can become reluctant to face the pain of others. Where to begin, particularly knowing that there is no feasible end in sight? Frequently enough we come to feel defeated by this. Belittled and perhaps even ashamed when we turn away from others, and disappointed or angry when we find others avoiding *us* in our suffering. When their judgments of us, either real or imagined, leave us feeling insignificant if not also impotent.

Rilke's poem, though, points us in an altogether different direction. He senses that the losses in life need not diminish us, at least if we heed his final injunction: "*You must change your life.*" His image of Apollo points to the god's strength precisely in and through what he has already lost. His call to change offers a different way of facing ourselves, not with enervating remorse because of our past or with an optimism toward a future time when things might be better, but precisely now, in the troubled present of our brokenness. In the pain of our losses and the crucible of our grief. Yes, here, in the fleeting now, you *can* change your life, even if you cannot repair what is broken or restore what is lost. What you carry within yourself is trust in your becoming.

*

Rilke's vision of Apollo points to a different view of wholeness than we often consider. One that has little to do with holding onto something we fear losing—a trusted relationship, perhaps, or a good job; status in our community; the respect of others. Perhaps what ultimately matters is being able to see *what is left*, however broken we might be; to recognize the strength that remains in the midst of our losses; to remember that all this points to the "whole" self we can never lose.

What Rilke accomplishes in this sonnet invites us to change the way we look at ourselves.

The call to gaze upon the incomplete torso of Apollo—the god of poetry and music and healing, after all—is a call to participate in the larger energies of change in our world. And change is one of the great motifs found throughout Rilke's poetry across the arc of his life. It is the call to you see how *your* change contributes to that larger whole, in whatever measures you take to embrace it. It is the call to participate in transforming the world by creatively beginning—again...and again...and again.

As Rilke put it in a letter written during the eventual depression he experienced in the aftermath of World War I, and the deep and stubborn distress that followed, "If [your] angel condescends to come, it will be because you have persuaded him, not with your tears, but by your humble decision to start afresh: *to be a beginner!*" In the moment of this beginning, when you find the courage to "start afresh," to begin again and thereby begin to live into change, you'll likely sense that the creative flow of your life—your active participation in your own life—is happening not only *within* you, but *through you.*

*

In the mid-1980s, the Southern novelist Reynolds Price wrote a stirring memoir entitled *A Whole New Life: An Illness and a Healing.* In it he tells the story of his anguishing struggle with spinal cancer, a disease that had come on suddenly in the height of his life and eventually required severe treatments that led to the permanent paralysis of his lower body. In telling the story of his unexpected—and undesired—journey through this illness, he began to find a new sense of what wholeness was all about, despite having forever lost the use of his legs.

In the course of his healing, he came to look differently at his own life, and begin to sense the "wholeness" he had never lost, though it was no longer outwardly visible. He began to see his life in terms not of who (or how) he had *been*, but of who he was *becoming*. He tells of the moment when he realized he'd moved from the unanswerable and finally debilitating question, *"Why did this loss happen to me?"* to the one that truly mattered: *"What am I to make of my whole life now?"*

His story is one brimming with wisdom, underscoring the courage it takes to live *forward* into what life still holds rather than *backward* with anger or regret at what had been lost. It reflects the wisdom of living into what it means that we are always, in every moment and each day of our lives, at the edge of new beginnings. For we are not simply the balance of our past. In the present, in *this* present, we carry the unknowable measure of our becoming—for *we are the future.*

*

Rilke stayed close to the wisdom of this discovery throughout his life. In a letter to a friend written a year after he published this poem, he suggests that "a failure should *not* be seen as a disappointment for those who begin by taking on an extreme challenge, refusing to settle for a goal of more modest proportions; this has to do with the specific measure of our undertakings, and has nothing to do with our sentiments nor should it discourage our efforts that are constituted, after all, from a thousand new beginnings."

A thousand new beginnings? What an invitation this is! Rilke is sure that *these* define us more significantly than do our endings, with all their failures, which after all are inevitable and belong in their own way to our growth. In this matter he is intent on encouraging those who might otherwise settle for a false security that diminishes us to avoid risking what might fail. *You must change your life.*

The sculptors of antiquity often portrayed Apollo, the god of music and dance, of prophecy and poetry, as carrying a lyre. They envisioned him as one ready to make music to lift the burdens of those who were suffering. To comfort them with melodies. To heal them with the beauty of song. Can you see him, this armless torso, still cradling that lyre in his arms? Can you hear from this headless torso a distant echo of the song

he sings for you? Can you imagine how he woos you, in your discour-
agement, with the sweet sound of his music? If not, then yes: *"You must
change your life."* And you *can.*

*

Rilke understood his vocation as a poet as this: the act of being able and
willing "to speak one's self," as he put it. When we give ourselves to this
work—of articulating our life—we become poets, regardless of whether
we write a single line. When you hear the call to "change your life," and
turn toward what awaits you in your future, you begin to come alive to
who you *are* as a whole self. You begin to see yourself as a "maker," the
English word for the simple Greek verb *"poiein"* from which we derive
the word "poet."

Becoming a poet means coming alive to who you are. It means
inhabiting the wholeness of who you are. It calls you to become fully
alive moment by moment in your life. In a letter of 1907 written to his
wife, the sculptor Clara Westhoff, Rilke said: "We live our lives so poorly
because we are always incomplete when we come to the present, incapa-
ble, and distracted by everything."

Poems, whether in our writing or reading them, offer a path of becom-
ing *more* complete. More *whole.* And this often has as much—or more—
to do with what the poem does not say but gestures toward, as in what
the poet asserts: "...because here there is no place / that doesn't see you."
Our change might begin with a poem like this, but that transformation
happens *in us* as we find ourselves invited to claim our "whole new life."

We turn to a poem like this one not to learn about Rilke's life but
hoping to find truer meaning in our own. And this happens not within
the *poem,* but within our own consciousness. How poems live within
us depends upon our willingness to open ourselves to them. *"You must
change your life."* Again, this is not an imperative, not an admonition; it is
an invitation. It invites us to risk seeing differently, which itself is a new
beginning that can change us.

What Rilke sees when gazing on the dismembered torso of Apollo is that wholeness is visible to be glimpsed in and with the brokenness, the partially destroyed, the often never-to-be-fixed. It is our imagination, and imaginative empathy, that opens us to experience how we belong to a deep wholeness that is always present, even in the midst of brokenness—for Rilke, standing before that statue, and for us as we gaze upon our own life.

Rilke expressed this in a letter to a friend written late in his own life as his final illness pressed upon him, taking away his strength and darkening his sense of the future: "In life one cannot awaken often enough the sense of a beginning within oneself. There is so little external change needed for that since *we actually transform the world from within our hearts*. If the heart longs for nothing but to be new and expansive, the world is instantly the same as on the day of its creation and infinite."

To transform the world from within your heart: this is the source and soul of our creative life. It is where we find new beginnings when we lose our way. The sense that, yes, *you are the future*, is where your creativity opens you to live in a forward direction. This is the conviction that gave voice to Rilke's deepest trust, not in some divine power "beyond" us, and not in hoping for a benevolent will that might influence us for the better. Rather, it points to the discovery each of us must make that we carry the power of transformation within us. It startles you in those moments when you realize that, yes, *you are the future*.

Where does this begin? Where and how do you find your calling in this life? Rilke simplifies the complexities that obscure such questions by pointing to your deepest desire—*to let your heart long to be new and expansive*. This is the work of creativity happening in you and through you toward others. When this begins to happen, when you choose to risk discovering that you are much more than your successes or your failures, you begin to become most truly yourself. You begin to live into the wholeness of what your life is calling you to *become*. This is not simply a matter of waiting for something new to come; it is the call to live into who you already are, and how you belong to a larger wholeness that gathers all that is broken: *You must change your life*.

*

Self-doubt is surely one of the most common and crippling of psychological burdens. It makes us mistrust our choices, our judgments, other people with their mixed motives—and ourselves. Children, in their youngest years, know little about it. We acquire it, however, as we grow older, when the tumble of inner questions begins: *Do I measure up? Am I good enough? Am I worthy? Am I lovable? Do I matter?* Of course, such questions point to our longing to be accepted and loved.

I know this. You know this. We realize that the shadow-side of this desire is our fear of rejection, our worry about not belonging, our shame about not being *longed for.* All of which can bring on a persistent sense of unworthiness. We may feel insecure about our entitlement to choose life, to have a particular point-of-view, even to be alive given the burdens we face in life—or those others close to us must carry.

Self-doubt need not be confused with healthy self-questioning and resilience rather than resistance about "being wrong." Painful versions of self-doubt, though, can be all too pervasive, except in egregiously narcissistic or "entitled" persons. Left unchecked, self-doubt can lead to shame which may cripple our ability to function, to say nothing of choking our creativity.

We may begin to see others not simply as smarter or stronger or more beautiful or handsome, but as *better.* And sooner or later we may well begin to feel not simply "less" than others, but unworthy or incapable of creating the inner as well as outer life we intend or desire to live. Self-doubt easily becomes self-disparagement, which can lead to social isolation—and loneliness, the painful and potentially destructive underside of Rilke's *Einsamkeit,* a chosen "solitude" or "inwardness" that is essential to reflection and creativity. When setbacks accumulate, or genuine encouragement from others is in short supply, this can trigger self-destructive behavior like addictions, eating disorders, suicidal tendencies, self-harm, recklessness, violence toward self and others, or a kind of "giving up" that takes you away from joy as well as risk.

One of the incubators of this in recent decades is the seductive world of online platforms. Social media, of course, did not create this problem. *We* carry the problem within us. These platforms simply allow such fears to be exploited, throwing fuel on the fire of our vulnerabilities. Someone ridicules us—or others—online for something we did, or failed to do, and the wound of humiliation and self-doubt grows.

While the methods of ridicule have become more public, as have the means of intimidation, a fear has grown of being singled out and diminished by others; of being casually dismissed as a loser, as someone who doesn't shine in terms of status or achievement. The pain this brings can readily damage your crucial sense of self and self-respect. It can plunge you into feelings of loss, isolation, desolation, or even prolonged anxiety or depression.

Perhaps these taunts exist only in your own mind and are not part of others' thinking. That doesn't make them less intrusive. You may begin to internalize assumed or actual negative judgments to the point that the critic within you has its way with your mind, leading to think that *I'm not as good—or talented or important—as others are. However hard I try, I won't stand out or be noticed.* We learn this way of being already as young children and may spend the rest of our lives trying to deal with the spiraling shame and self-doubt that drive it. These tragic social habits are worsened when bullies in a "crowd" make fun of those they regard as particularly vulnerable based on gender, sexual orientation, race, social class, or dis/ability.

Children learn from their family of origin at least as powerfully as from their peers, yet it is often among their peers that petty or cruel bias or prejudice is lived out. The problem with this spiral, if left unchecked, is that it starts to eat away at your soul. Fearing being disliked by others, you may begin to dislike yourself; fearing failure, you may shrink your world to what feels manageable. Anxious that you'll not attain the successes you presumed would come—or others expected of you—you begin to become fearful, or even bitter. You might even resist learning something new or taking on difficult tasks out of fear that you won't succeed. Or shine.

*

Rilke's poem about Apollo is one about re-membering what was dis-membered. It is a poem that re-minds us of the wholeness that "shines" like the god's lost eyes from an inner vision. Such a vision is not a statement of duty—*"You must...change..."*—but rather a glimpse of possibility, in this case that of seeing our inner connectedness to the "Whole," even in the presence of loss. This sense of belonging reminds us that we all are part of this larger wholeness—in and through our failings and imperfections. Yours, too, with all your losses and fears, is a "whole new life." For *you are the future.*

CHAPTER 7

INWARDNESS

I believe in all that has never yet been said.
I want to free my most intimate feelings;
what no one has ever dared desire
will suddenly become my nature.

If this is too bold, my God, forgive me.
But with this I want to tell you
that my noblest power should be an instinct,
and thus without anger and without hesitation—
this is how children cherish you.

With this flood, with this flow
into the broad arms of the open sea,
with this expansive return,
I want to bear witness to you; I want to proclaim you
like none before.

And if this is pride, then let me be proud
in my prayer,
which stands so earnest and alone
before your shadowed brow.

—from *The Book of Hours*

[*STEPHANIE DOWRICK*]

It's with somewhat mixed emotions that I want to suggest that if religion or spirituality is to have any point at all, then it is to free us from any thinking or dogma that would make us smaller, more shut-in, or more frightened than we need to be.

For all that, I readily acknowledge it is a brave person who can easily or fully bear the fragility and uncertainty that is at the heart of mortal existence. Fundamentalisms of all kinds actively discourage *living into the questions*. Or even raising them. Instead, they provide fully guaranteed "answers." That strikes me as an immense loss because consciousness is itself never static. As conscious beings, we have moment-by-moment chances to expand rather than contract our inner horizons, as well as in the way we view what we call "the world."

Reading poetry such as Rilke's offers individual readers leaps of awareness, as well as glimpses of a far, far bigger world than fundamentalism describes—outside as well as "inside." Yet it is indisputable that the speed of change in our century is unprecedented. It has become terrifyingly difficult to know which sources of information are worthy of our trust. Our healthiest instincts for good, kindness, or beauty, are too frequently thwarted by indifference. Or worse. Something more than understanding is needed for those whose circumstances or conditioning have led them to cling to a fragile raft of absolutism amid a vast ocean of unknowing. This extends to education, too, about which most people have strong opinions. "Education" may include the way you have been taught or trained to view poetry: as a portal to a freer view, or as entirely peripheral to what "matters" or to what is most predictable.

Poetry, when it is real, can never be predictable; cannot be replicated by AI; has to express something raw, freshly born from human experience, delivered from the senses as well as the intellect, anarchic in the real meaning of that word. Brazilian educator Paulo Freire makes a lot of sense to me with his statement, "There's no such thing as neutral education. Education functions as an instrument to bring about either conformity or freedom." Across a century, I am imagining a big hurrah from Rilke to that sentiment.

*

Because of my mother's early death from cancer during my child-hood—an event that has shaped my life from that moment to this—and because of the complex post-war recovery times I lived through, my early life was sufficiently unpredictable that I had no choice but to know that's what life is: fragile, mortal, miraculous. For some questions, there are no answers. A strange "advantage"? Yes, possibly, but at an awful cost.

In adulthood, however, with at least some sense of inner continuity and of a perspective that travels backwards and forward, the shedding of a need *to know everything*, or to demand that tomorrow will be very much like today—or better still, like a romanticized "yesterday"—is to be inwardly liberated. Liberated not only from fear but also from the anxiety and tension that build rapidly when you refuse the push, the impetus, the *mystery* of life itself. No one can achieve this for you. You, though, can achieve this for yourself.

The Zen tradition in its many forms has something to add here—in ways that Rilke could not have intellectually anticipated. Bernie Glassman is a former Zen teacher and profound peace and humanitarian activist. He had this to say: "When we bear witness to the unfolding of our daily lives, not shrinking from any situation that arises, we learn. We open to what is. And in that process, a healing arises."

A healing arises. The *how* and *when* of inner liberation, of course, will always be relative and highly subjective. I would strongly suggest it is also dependent on an active acceptance of inwardness, a world of inner sense which this book overtly encourages and which Rilke celebrates: *Ich glaube an Alles noch nie Gesagte…*, "I believe in all that has never yet been said." What a marvelously inverted credo this is. "I believe…" not in what I have been taught to recite or what has emerged from other people's certainties, but *in all that has never yet been said.*

Perhaps those "things" are unsayable. Of all literary forms, poetry carries us into this terrain of the unsayable and even unknowable, taking us almost as far as music can. Or the quiet contemplation of nature, of which we are a part. Words for inwardness can run short. In 1913, as Europe began its trek toward the insane horrors of world war, Rilke wrote of *"innigstes unser"*—our innermost being—as something exceeding our everyday grasp, perhaps something that can only be alluded to, somehow sensed, or "taken in" as if by instinct.

Yet surely the continuing and growing interest in Rilke in our times, when poetry is far too often dismissed as trivial or irrelevant, speaks volumes for a longing in so many of us to leave behind our flailing attempts at certainty and to trust in *beyond, more than, ripeness, inner-ness*—even when this will frequently elude us:

> I believe in all that has never yet been said.
> I want to free my most intimate feelings;
> what no one has ever dared desire
> will suddenly become my nature.
>
> If this is too bold, my God, forgive me.
> But with this I want to tell you
> that my noblest power should be an instinct,
> and thus without anger and without hesitation—
> this is how children cherish you.

To free your *most intimate feelings*; to feel the desire, the *necessity* of that; to want your *noblest power* to become so natural it is no longer subject to decisions but becomes as easy as an *instinct*, as a child's unselfconscious impulse: all of this is to honor what is so specific about human consciousness and its potentials. To claim your whole self is a mighty thing, a "bold" thing to quote the adjective used above.

To claim consciousness as your inheritance and right can also be transformative. Perhaps the very act of claiming is already transformative. I'd like to think so.

The late American poet and translator Robert Bly introduced many readers—including me—to the vigor of Rilke, to that specific sensuality and earthiness co-existent with his proximity to transcendence and capacity to convey it. It is Bly who pointed out that reading Rilke "can be a shock for readers used to public literature." In the introduction to his own *Selected Poems of Rainer Maria Rilke*, Bly suggests that "most American writers begin proudly, even aggressively, in the outer world. Rilke, though, begins elsewhere." Bly continues, "When I first read Rilke, in my twenties, I felt a deep shock upon realizing the amount of introversion he had achieved, and the adult attention he paid to inner states."

Bly's comments interest as well as move me. I would suggest that "the amount of introversion [Rilke] had achieved" was due more to his courage to preserve it rather than his attempt to achieve it—though perhaps these ultimately are the same thing. I would also note that one of Bly's less well-known books, published in 1997, is *The Sibling Society*, subtitled *An Impassioned Call for the Rediscovery of Adulthood*. Bly urges readers in that book to notice how much public and private discourse is childish, petulant, and obnoxiously self-serving. He points out that there is far more squabbling and point-scoring than listening or learning and that wisdom is neither commonly sought, nor easily found. Responsibility and accountability are what many of us are taught in kindergarten, then trained to subdue as we pass into adulthood.

Adolescence ought to be an interlude of a few years between childhood and adulthood. Bly makes a compelling case that it is where many—too many—remain stuck and regressed. What this means is that a person's ego remains too weak to be willingly accountable or responsible. For whatever is wrong, "others" are to blame, and what Jung called the shadow—that Bly also wrote of—remains disowned so that denied levels of self-disgust are projected onto those who fit the bill of "inferior" in the dangerously stunted adult's view, and psyche.

*

Poetry of any fair caliber demands a degree of inwardness that must simultaneously draw on patient reflection while resisting any pull toward sentimentality. It must face into, face up to "terror" as well as beauty. Humility needs oxygen, as does quiet persistence—and a belief that the bigger picture is evolving, neither static nor self-evident. A different poem from Rilke's *The Book of Images* ends with these lines:

> Victories don't entice him.
> His growth is this: to be one deeply defeated
> by an ever greater one.

In many of Rilke's poems, including those we have drawn on, the poet calls us to a larger view than could ever be gained by an anxiety-driven need to be "better than," or "best." When I discuss my interest in Rilke with those who know little or nothing about his work, I realize how difficult it is to convey that a poet so closely associated with the "visionary" is also radical in his appreciation and vivifying of "things," rather than in reifying human beings. He is radical, too, in his consistent refusals of conventionality as well as self-diminishment, in his work and life. His view of the world, and most particularly our place within it, equally rejects the tugs of the known, the expected, the "pleasing."

> With this flood, with this flow
> into the broad arms of the open sea,
> with this expansive return,
> I want to bear witness to you; I want to proclaim you
> like none before.
>
> And if this is pride, then let me be proud
> in my prayer,
> which stands so earnest and alone
> before your shadowed brow.

The "face" of God, with its "shadowed brow," *is* hidden to us. "Whatever we can say God is, God is not," declared the Christian mystic Meister

Eckhart. Yet the "shadowed" Divine is nonetheless the direction of our most ardent seeking—for wholeness, wellness, oneness.

*

Inwardness, in other words, suggests more than a state of mind. It is a recognition of consciousness and of consciousness's depth; of the reality of *your* depth and of our shared need for seeking and meaning. A refusal to know or heed any degree of inwardness is to condemn yourself to a surface-life that may entrench a lifelong immaturity. To our collective grave cost, that is what the vast majority of Westerners are persuaded to accept as normal. Hyper-extroversion is demanded and given. Hyper-activity in the cause of commerce wins high praise and rewards. Yet when inwardness is mocked or actively discouraged, or seeking at depth is scorned or dismissed as "elite," that risks making you more compliant than you need to be. And smaller: "with this flow / into the beckoning arms of the open ocean..."

Oddly, and wonderfully, science may come to our rescue here. (Science in the service of poetry: how perfect.) Especially science as interpreted by those who know that it works by multiplying questions amid "expanding universes," or amid an expanding *understanding* of what "universe" could mean to the mind of a mystic, a poet, or the archetypal "fool" urging us toward a greater delight in life, along with seriousness.

In 2002, American science and nature writer and journalist Tim Folger was asking the famed American theoretical physicist John Wheeler, "Why does the universe exist?" More recently, in December 2023, particle physicist Brian Cox—public "face" of science in the UK—was addressing the same question, with the astonishing cosmological discoveries of the last two decades to further inform him. At the Sydney Opera House, with images from the Hubble and the James Webb Space telescopes together with live symphonic music as support, Cox gave a mesmerizing tour of the vast cosmology in which our planet—and our lives—exist. Among his comments came this startling call:

As far we can tell, it is possible, it is plausible, that this planet is the only island of meaning in an ocean of 400 billion suns…and therefore if we destroy this through inaction or deliberate action then we may eliminate meaning in a galaxy of 400 billion stars, potentially forever. I do think we have to take it seriously that this world—this precious world—might be the only place for millions or even billions of light years in every direction where there are collections of atoms that can think and feel and do science and write music and bring meaning to an otherwise meaningless universe. And, therefore, it might be our responsibility alone to ensure that there is a future for life and meaning out there amongst the stars.

Yes, indeed, "…*it might be our responsibility alone to ensure that there is a future for life and meaning out there amongst the stars.*" How extraordinary, how thrilling it is to be brought by these most recent advances into a truer understanding of the hints that are everywhere in Rilke's vision and writing.

These are hints—and sometimes more than hints—of our potential inner immensity, correlating to an outer immensity far beyond anything most of us could imagine, never mind what could have been rationally conceived of in early 20th-century life. In less than a hundred years, and, with some discoveries, in less than a decade, cosmology has revealed the reality of an outer universe, alluded to so richly and diversely—so boldly—by this profound poet of the "inner spaces." And what are these "inner spaces" but a pointer to the "beyond" *where we also belong?*

> With this flood, with this flow
> into the broad arms of the open sea,
> with this expansive return,
> I want to bear witness to you; I want to proclaim you
> like none before.

*

Why does the universe exist? Friedrich Nietzsche—a near-contemporary of Rilke and an ardent admirer of Lou Andreas-Salomé—asked this question a little differently: "How can humanity justify our existence?" Brian Cox took this up, claiming that "the only interesting question in all of philosophy is, 'What does it mean to live a finite, fragile life in an infinite, eternal and, frankly, very strange universe?'"

We circle back to the temptations of certainty, then away again.

This is the realm of philosophy as well as science. And of true poetry. Yet, there is also something touchingly natural about this question, *Why does the universe exist?* It is one that absorbs the mind even of young children when their curiosity is not dampened by banalities. It is also one that each of us can return to in a purely personal way throughout our lives because it so directly corresponds with those innermost questions of all: *Why do I exist? Does my life have meaning?*

Cox affirms that each of us is "a collection of atoms"—and thus "related" to the stars—yet, as he says, "those atoms [human beings] can think, can do science, write symphonies [and poetry]." In this he echoes lines from one of Rilke's *Sonnets to Orpheus:* "With words and gestures, little by little, / we make the world our own" (I.16).

*

It is easy to over-work the adjective "profound." When it comes to understanding (or just glimpsing) the singular potentials and responsibilities of human consciousness, however, the exalted vision of being that these new discoveries give us cannot be described in any other way. It was American theoretical physicist John Wheeler's earlier insight that the quest for an answer to that central question *Why does the universe exist?* inevitably entails wrestling with the implications of one of the strangest aspects of modern physics. According to the rules of quantum mechanics, *our observations influence the universe at the most fundamental levels.*

In Rilke's work, we find the immensities of "out there" paralleled "in here." The boundary between an objective world beyond us and our own subjective consciousness *blurs* in quantum mechanics. As Rilke wonders in one of the late *Duino Elegies*, "Earth, isn't it this that you long for: to rise *invisibly* within us?" For as journalist John Folger explains: "When physicists look at the basic constituents of reality— atoms and their innards, or the particles of light called photons—*what they see depends on how they have set up their experiment.… From the quantum perspective the universe is an extremely interactive place*" [my italics].

*

Is it too much of a stretch, then, to ascribe something of a "quantum view" to a contemporary reading of Rilke—and, through this, of our own lives? We know that the poet viewed art as a "cosmic, creative, transforming force." He also endorsed art's power to "change the normal world," by which he surely meant the world as it is routinely and too often narrowly seen; art, embodied, *within* life. "I do not want to tear art from life," he wrote. "I know that somehow and somewhere both belong together."

Reading Rilke—taking in a phrase, a whole poem, or an idea expressed in prose or a letter—opens realms that moved him instinctively, including those we think of as belonging to our individual and collective "uncertainties." As our awareness or consciousness is shifted, if not changed, we are changed, *and so is our world*. Listen again, to the visionary voice of this complex man who was "to his bones" a poet. Say the words aloud if you can. They belong to you as much as they do to anyone.

> I believe *in all that has never yet been said* [my italics].
> I want to set free my most intimate feelings;
> what no one has ever dared desire
> will suddenly become my nature.

A century later, the popular understanding of consciousness remains limited. So does our understanding of the cosmos. The synergizing of ideas from both philosophy and physics—when naturally mediated through poetry—takes us forward. How clearly that matters. "I believe in [what] is not yet said." Even as we mark the astounding discoveries of science in our own lifetimes, we can marvel at the intuitions of Rilke.

By resisting the urgency of premature answers, poetic thinking—like the most marginal comprehension of what physics and cosmology bring you—can mightily encourage you to be *with* your deepest thinking, your most honest self-enquiry, your search for meaning, perhaps coming to accept that some questions will outlive you, even while they strengthen your relationship to life *as you live them.*

*

Rilke was not a scientist. Nor was he a mystic. Not as it was understood in his time and not as it is understood in ours. It is indisputable, though, that as a poet he repeatedly tapped into concepts far bigger than were common, extending his "ways of seeing" far beyond himself. Just as physics does. Just as quantum mechanics does. Just as cosmology does. Poetry may seem an odd path toward a less certain, more embracing vision. It is one, however, that sometimes makes sudden and obvious sense.

This is most profoundly demonstrated through a glimpse of what Rilke called "the Open." When he wrote of this, as a kind of porousness to what is real, he did this not to try to persuade, much less convince readers. He despised anything that smacked of propaganda—or of pushing an ideology or belief. Rilke was himself seeking to understand or perhaps just experience the forces of the *unmanifest*, the *invisible*. "Who among the angelic orders would hear me if I cried out?" he asks in the first of his *Elegies*. In one of his *Sonnets to Orpheus* (II.1), come lines that glow:

> Solitary wave whose
> gradual sea I am;
> most frugal you of all possible seas, –
> gained-space.

How many of these places, with all their rooms, were already inside of me.

Dare we read Rilke or speak his words aloud in order to inch toward something like a "quantum view" ourselves—we who carry untold "places of spaces" within us? Can we, with a rediscovered fleetness of mind, run with something that so dramatically—and truthfully—brings our attention back to our shared cosmic questions, and to our own intimate, intense reflections?

As Rilke warns us in the *Elegies*, "For to stay [to remain fixed] is to be nowhere at all." How powerful that brief statement is. How powerful, too, that change—like paradox—is the very essence of life. A moment of perfection is simultaneously a moment of decay. An exquisite bunch of buds sitting in a jug or vase on your kitchen table shows this as first the buds open, then flowers show themselves in their unfolding glory even as their fading accelerates.

It is much the same with fruit, or vegetables, picked but not eaten in their prime. Our household mirror affirms the same story. So do our photo albums. Or scrolling through a decade of images on our phones. "Now" is itself a feast that cannot be held back. Sometimes "now" is a tyranny. Acknowledging that, and the truth of life's rhythms, enhances a connection to life. And where do we register this movement that connects us to every form of life? Inwardly. *Inwardly.*

"I want my noblest power [to] be an instinct...." With Rilke, with a quiet re-reading of that line, not unlike a vow, my response becomes a grateful and wholehearted "Yes."

*

For all the benefits of inwardness that this chapter celebrates, and Rilke's work amply demonstrates, a fear of inwardness that many adults have surely needs acknowledging. What also needs acknowledging is that entire generations are coming to maturity with little or no experience of the potential fullness of uncommitted time. Daydreaming, reverie, getting bored then going beyond boredom, are foreign experiences for many young and not-so-young with ready access to ear buds, tablets, cell phones 24/7. There are biological as well as psychological consequences to this change in everyday human behavior. "Inward" may increasingly seem like a direction in which few want to travel.

Rilke's need for and celebration of deep solitude and even deeper reflection is widely known. Yet in the lines that follow he shows compassion for those who fear "going inside." To Franz Kappus, the "young poet," he wrote,

> Do not be frightened if a sadness rises up before you greater than any you have seen so far; if a restiveness like light and cloud shadows passes over your hands and everything that you do. Let yourself know that something is happening within you, that life itself has not forgotten you, *that life holds you in its hand; it will not let you fall* [my italics]. Why do you want to exclude from your life any uneasiness, miseries, or depressions? For, after all, you do not [yet] know what work these experiences are doing within you.

Is it here that we have a striking inversion of the now-familiar call to "let everything happen, beauty and terror"? It is terror—confusion, isolation, desolation, chaos, and also death—that we understandably fear. Yet, in that fearing and recoiling, we may also close off to the depth of beauty that is within us as well as around and far beyond us. Drawing up from that well of beauty regenerates us. May heal us. Sometimes, in the darkest or most confusing times, this "happens." Sometimes, we need consciously to make ourselves available to the possibility of an arising. Even in the presence of terror.

Any hymn to beauty praises life. All of life.

. . . I want to tell you

that my noblest power should be an instinct,
and thus without anger and without hesitation—
this is how children cherish you.

With this flood, with this flow
into the broad arms of the open sea,
with this expansive return,
I want to bear witness to you; I want to proclaim you
like none before.

Like none before.

CHAPTER 8

YOU ARE THE STILLNESS

My life is not this steep hour
in which you see me hurrying so.
I am a tree standing before what I once was;
I am only one of my mouths,
and, at that, the first to close.

I am the stillness between two notes
that don't easily harmonize,
because the note Death wants to lift itself up ...

But in the dark interval both come,
trembling, to join as one...
                    and the song remains beautiful.

                    —from *The Book of Hours*

[*MARK S. BURROWS*]

"I am the stillness..." What a strange, unexpected confession this is. It seems to call for an indrawing of breath, even a quieting of mind, to read such words. What might happen if you claimed this for yourself? If you imagined, in the midst of all your unsettling fears and distressing worries, that *you are the stillness*? What seems unavoidable is the pressured "hour" we face, which seems anything but "still" given the 24/7 society we inhabit, with its ever-accelerating pressures and accumulating demands. All of this exhausts us, awakening our longing for some sense of that stillness. But to presume to say, *I am the stillness?* Is such a claim even imaginable?

This poem was written a few years before Rilke's letters of advice to a "young poet" where he beckons him, and us as later readers, to "live the questions"—and, even more so, to "live everything." Now. Directly and boldly, it points to the difficult fate of those who live a hurried and demanding life, gripped by the pressures of what the poet describes as "this steep hour" in which we find ourselves rushing about.

A more likely sentiment that might come to mind is the complaint of how pressed we feel. Rilke knew something of this, living as he did in an era of increasing motorization with its accelerating speed. And though Rilke had written those marvelous letters in his late 20s, they seem seasoned by a wisdom exceeding his years.

The demands that Rilke prefaced in this poem and faced in those letters, published after his death as *Letters to a Young Poet*, seem only to have intensified for readers over the intervening years, living as we now do in a culture saturated with an over-accessibility (and corresponding "under-availability") he could not have imagined.

It is a poem that does not so much lament as simply register our difficulties at the outset, before suggesting through a string of images how we might reframe the questions we carry within us. Each time I turn to read this poem, I let the arc of its compressed story unfold slowly and quietly. It supports me in that central task of self-trust: *living the questions* I face in my life—the confusions, uncertainties, disappointments, shocks—with authenticity and courage. With a quiet confidence I don't always feel. It calls me to face what is unresolved, unfinished, broken in my own life as an inevitable part of who I am. Just as it is an inevitable part of who you are. Because often, too often, we find it difficult, even painful, to imagine that we are that "stillness" found between the competing pressures of our lives.

This poem evokes for us that sense of inner wholeness we long to experience. It calls us to face what is unsettled in our lives as a vital part of who each of us is—in our "becoming" from day to day. Not as a project we can complete once and for all, but more like a journey into greater calm. Into a more balanced consciousness.

Perhaps this is something we glimpse through dreams, those images that shape themselves deep in our unconscious. Or things we glimpse, at best, in those moments of reverie we sometimes feel when watching the clouds drift across a summer sky. When we hear children laughing as they play, somewhere just out of sight. When we find ourselves gazing upon some small miracle close at hand—observing a caterpillar inch its way along a branch or watching one of the last leaves quivering on a slender branch in an autumn wind. When we sense that somehow, amid all the rush, we belong to a deeper rhythm of life. That we somehow belong to all this.

Rilke writes of a "dark interval" in which the exhausting demands we face are harmonized. There are so many of these in our lives, though none greater than the existential one of life and death itself. And that shadowed interval? Is this where we must ultimately learn to face that gnawing anxiety that sometimes awakens us in the middle of the night? That "dark" moment which holds hidden within itself an experience of stillness, even if only momentary and seemingly remote, which is some-thing we long for? A gift we yearn to receive, knowing how the pressures of our lives so often deplete us of the restfulness we need—and desire—in order to survive, to say nothing of that greater longing to thrive that we carry deep within us?

The experience of reading a poem like this, quietly and repeatedly, is that it begins to bring the gentle rhythm of Rilke's voice closer to our own. I came upon it for the first time when I was much younger and could still imagine, with youthful naivete, that I could handle the pres-sures I already felt bearing down on me. Over the ensuing years, as the burdens multiplied, I began to find what it meant to make these words my own, speaking them quietly to myself, over and over again, until I knew them by heart.

As they became part of me, gathered in the gentle rhythm of my breathing, I began to discover them as an unexpected gift. As Rilke's words slowly became my own, even if I could imagine them only dimly in my own life, I sensed how these images might live within me—and how I might dwell within them. How the poem might become a guiding light in difficult and shadowed moments in my life. How it could offer a path forward through the complications that I already experienced and knew might well increase with time. As they did. I sensed, if only dimly, that as I faced what was "unresolved," not yet fully comprehended, not yet authentically "lived" in my own life, this poem could become a guiding presence. As it has done.

*

The first-person singular in Rilke's poems isn't his alone. It is yours, and mine; it is ours, reminding us that we belong to each other in our anxieties as in our longings:

> My life is not this steep hour
> in which you see me hurrying so.

Not this steep hour: the image is a startling one. No matter how life's demands bear down on us, they do not define the depth of our lives—which Rilke sometimes refers to as our "innerness." "Not this": no one's complex life—not yours, not mine—can be summoned in a single image, Rilke seems to be asserting. No one's multi-dimensional, unpredictable, precious life is "just" a stereotype, merely a piece of data or a brisk sum of all its "parts." What makes us fully human is unquantifiable. It embraces not only what we have been, but what we are becoming—for we carry the future always within ourselves. It is mysterious, even to us. Often especially so.

When I first came upon this poem, I began to memorize it—as if instinctively—in Rilke's German, internalizing its beautiful cadences with their lyrical flow. As I did, I began to experience moments of insight in what felt like an electric current coursing through me. His words began to become my own as if he named something important that I already knew.

Yet this happened gradually. At the start, I simply felt "named" by the blunt force of the opening lines, pointing as they do to the experience of "hurriedness" I knew in my life. The tumble of metaphors that followed, however, struck me—initially at least—as strange. Even confusing. I sensed, though, before I could put words on it, that the poet was here framing a deep, existential question I could not resolve on my own: Who am I, caught within the pressures of my life? What is the source of that "stillness" that I feel dwelling beneath the surging restlessness of my heart?

As if to heighten the strangeness, Rilke turns in the poem's third line to a startling image when he suggests that "*I am a tree.*" To which he adds, "I am a tree *standing before what I once was.*" My life, and yours, is not simply what we feel on the outside, or even in terms of the internal pressures that so often seem to overpower us. I am rooted. You are rooted, even when you and I don't feel it. We are grounded in this earth despite—and precisely in the midst of—all the swirling demands that press upon us. The question is, how do we find that sense of groundedness?

*

Another poet writing in the early 19th century, John Keats, spoke of this as well. He suggested—as mentioned above—that the truest response to the uncertainty we face is not to seek resolution. Not to try to "fix" it, but to live into it. The poet spoke of this with a strange phrase, describing it as "negative capability." By this he pointed to our need to let go of our desire to control; to manage; to demand. For we are also, Keats knew, "capable of being in uncertainties, Mysteries, doubts, without any irritable reaching after fact and reason." We have the strength to face what is unresolved, though this calls for honesty and compassion—toward ourselves and others. For we are all more than all that we know. *For we are all the future.*

This is another way of understanding what Rilke meant by "living the questions."

He knew how difficult it was to accept "uncertainties" as a vital part of our identity, as an element of openness in our lives. He struggled with this throughout his life, often tormented with self-doubt and worried about his dependence on others. In addressing the anxieties his young correspondent—and we—face, he emphasized the courage it takes to ground ourselves *where we are*. And in who we are. And to do so not in terms of the duties we face or the demands that press upon us, but at the deeper and truer core of our being. In the depths of our "innerness": "*I am the stillness.*"

Today, as we read this poem more than a century since Rilke wrote it in 1899, we find ourselves in an age when many of us are broadly defined by the externals of work, relationship status, income bracket, age, and physical appearance—as well as the bigger markers of race, sexuality, gender, nationality, and class. But what Rilke draws attention to transcends all these measures of "difference." He is pointing to something more essential, an underlying truth that grounds us in all this.

The startling image he draws on here offers an example of what this might look like: "*I am a tree standing before what I once was.*" We are rooted not where we once *were*, but where we now stand. Despite what might still be, or feel, unresolved in our life. We are grounded in the midst of the multitude of experiences and interactions we know, and in the way we relate to ourselves, to others, and, in and through all this, to this earth we share. "I am a tree," grounded in this time and place and in the "innerness" of the one I truly am, "standing before what I once was."

Imagining your life as such a tree may seem initially strange. Even uncomfortable. After all, we live in a society driven by motion, status, self-importance. It echoes, though, a more ancient image: that of the *axis mundi*, that "axis of the earth," the grounding-point which ancient peoples viewed as the stabilizing center of the world. A tree, unmoving and quite simply *there*. The contrast of this line stands in stark contrast to the hurried beginning, ringing with Rilke's conviction—stated at the outset—that "my life is *not* this steep hour...."

The French philosopher, Gaston Bachelard, once wrote that "all great, simple images reveal a psychic state." All outer images point to something deep within us; they mirror things in the soul. What would it take for you to claim this, against the hurrying tides that press against you and take from you the peace you long for? Rilke offers another image of what this might mean, declaring:

> I am only one of my mouths,
> and, at that, the first to close.

What does it mean that our truest self is not to be found in how we speak or what we say, but in who we are—in and through but also beyond our speech?

Rilke knew that there may be many "mouths" in our lives, in the relational postures we take because of our outward identity. This may be because of how we identify ourselves or find ourselves identified by others—in terms of race/ethnicity, gender/sexual orientation, or cultural/social status. Or because of our functional identity as parent, partner, colleague, friend.

Which is the real *me*, the true *you*? Rilke points to the part of you that is willing to keep silent, to pause, to relinquish control, to refuse to criticize. "To be capable of being in uncertainties, Mysteries, doubts." To remain grounded in *unknowing*. Rooted in simply "being-here," which Rilke often gestured toward with the poignant German word *Dasein*. He points to how our true self waits for us in the place where we choose silence over chatter, solitude over the crowd, composure over reactivity, creativity over predictability.

Those other "mouths"—yours or those of others—suggest expectations you might have for yourself, or those others have placed upon you, whether in real or imagined ways. They suggest the obligations of an "inflated self," of a managed self, the one that takes on far too much and forgets about the self-care that opens us to the deeper truth of simply being-here. And being-ourselves-here. The one that is so often overwhelmed with that "steep hour" in which the demands of others press down hard on us.

*

In his *Little Book on the Human Shadow*, the poet and early translator of Rilke, Robert Bly, writes out of his own struggles that "if any help was going to arrive to lift me out of my misery, it would come from the dark side of my personality." He also names the internal splitting that can divide us from ourselves in a world that can be relentlessly judgmental, and often idiotic in the superficiality of its judging criteria:

> Our culture teaches us from early infancy to split and polarize dark and light, which I call here "mother" and "father." So some people admire the right-thinking, well-lit side of the personality, and that group one can associate with the father, if one wants to; and some admire the left-thinking, poorly-lit side, and that group one can associate with the mother, if one wants to, and mythologically with the Great Mother. Most artists, poets, and musicians belong to the second group and love intuition, music, the feminine, owls, and the ocean. The right-thinking group loves action, commerce, and Empire.

Rilke sensed that polarities were always with us, and within us—light and dark; good and bad; right and wrong—and that our work was that of integrating them. Finding ways, in the "dark interval" that they construct, to bring them into relation to each other:

> But in the dark interval both come,
> trembling, to join as one...

What if your authentic, if often ignored, "self" depends upon embracing the tensions in your life? And, when things fall apart, to see that falling as a necessary condition of growth? This is the transformative, self-compassionate, and self-respectful insight that *living the questions* brings, that pausing "in the dark interval" offers, that openness for reflection and self-compassion invites.

These commitments to hold the tensions, and not our tendencies to control, enable us to allow the outer structures to fall apart, as they must, to make room to discover a larger, truer self. This is what a "quick fix" can never accomplish. As Rilke knew, and as we must discover again and again in our lives. In the stanza that follows, Rilke continues to explore the need to discover the harmonies that are truer than what feels discordant in our lives. This goes deeper than a "self-help" strategy. It penetrates to the mystery of our "self," refusing to let us linger in practiced self-evasion.

> I am the stillness between two notes
> that don't easily harmonize.

What are those two "notes"? One, as the poet is quick to say, is "Death" that refuses to disappear, that "wants to lift itself up"; the other, he infers, is life, that wellspring of experience with all its unsettled and, often enough, unsettling dimensions. His approach echoes the wisdom of the ancient Hebrew scripture: "I have set before you life and prosperity, death and adversity. . .[and] life and death, blessings and curses. Choose life so that you and your descendants may live" (Deuteronomy 30:15, 19).

Rilke is not settling with Hamlet's despairing quandary, "to be or not to be." His urging is not for mere survival, though sometimes that is all we seem capable of managing. No, he goes further in imagining what it means to thrive, which is an experience we long for at a deeper depth of our being—in our "innerness," beyond the restlessness and anxiety we often feel. He senses that finding our way to thriving depends on integrating the competing tensions in our lives, not trying to manage or control them. "I am a tree standing before what I once was."

What this means is both simple and demanding at once. Rilke is not content to say that we bear stillness within us, at the heart of who we are. He goes further to say, *You are the stillness* itself. How far this is from the temptation we all face to externalize our life, chasing about as we often do in the hope of finding such a sense of quiet *outside* ourselves. Rilke goes to the depths of our "innerness" when he reminds us to look for that stillness *within* our life. To find our way to the mystery that we *are* this stillness, that our essential identity rests in that place where the tensions coexist within us. Where we embrace all that feels unresolved within our lives—and listen for it like the quiet space in a musical performance between two notes that seem in tension with each other.

> I am the stillness between two notes
> that don't easily harmonize,
> because the note Death wants to lift itself up...

*

What is "Death"? This is among the greatest questions of all that face us. It is the deep mystery that invites us to *live*—here and now—in this often "dark interval." Rilke was wise enough, even as a young poet, to know that there was no set answer to find here. All that we can be sure of is that death is inevitable for each of us. But the how, when, where, and even why of it remain for all of us the biggest unknown. It is part of your becoming, the hidden voice reminding you that *you are the future.*

It is also, perhaps, the largest of the many uncertainties in our lives. When Rilke suggests that "the note Death wants to lift itself up," he is inviting you to lean into life's shadows. To embrace the ambiguities of your life. To face the contradictions that exist within you, in addition to the conflicts of our world as well as that maze of tensions that inevitably arise between yourself and others. He is inviting you to see that no matter how fiercely you live into all this, past and present, death *will* "lift itself up." In the moment of that realization, you find yourself invited to affirm that life—*your* life—is more and not less precious for this. That *you are the future.*

What you long for, what we all long for, is to indwell the stillness at the heart of the tensions and contradictions in our lives, and in death itself. And to experience that stillness, which the poet knew as the primary source of life; as the heartbeat of regenerative creativity; as the source of a new clarity. As another way of framing the compelling Buddhist notion of "coming awake" to life—in the face of all the uncertainties, including above all our own death.

In the third of his letters to Franz Kappus, Rilke wrote:

> Allow your judgments their own quiet, undisturbed development, which like every measure of progress arise from deep within you and can be neither forced nor hurried. Everything is about carrying and then giving birth. To live as an artist, in your understanding and in your creative life, depends on letting each impression and each seed of a feeling come to completion, entirely in itself, in the dark, in the unsayable, in the unconscious, beyond the reach of one's own understanding, and with deep humility and patience to wait for the hour when a new clarity is born.

As Rilke knew, as you also know, creativity is about embracing *everything*. It calls us to *live* everything in our lives, "beauty and terror" as he elsewhere puts it.

It is about seeing "each impression and each seed of a feeling"—the pleasant along with the unpleasant, the easy together with the difficult—as holding the potential of growth, of change, of transformation. A mighty old oak begins with a small acorn that can be held in the palm of your hand. A great painting of Van Gogh began in the countless hours he spent learning to draw, and eventually practicing with colors, and he kept painting even when no one noticed his talent or affirmed the beauty of his canvases.

Here, Rilke reminds us, we must learn to be content with creating, even if no one notices. Even if *we* ourselves do not understand what it is all about. Ours is not the work of arriving, but of journeying; not of creating a finished product but of contributing each of the brushstrokes, one by one—however small and simple—that we are able to make. And then, "with deep humility and patience," we are to "wait for the hour when a new clarity" will be born anew within us, above all in that "dark interval" where the competing tensions in our lives begin to resolve into the deeper harmony whose powers we always carry within ourselves.

The Japanese know this as the practice of "kaizen," which literally means "change–good," an insight rooted in the wisdom that change comes "step by step," incrementally, as we live into a greater sense of the wholeness we desire.

For those of us accustomed to the acoustic range of western music, that "stillness" is something we somehow *feel* even when we cannot explain it in musicological terms. We sense it when confronted with a musical "seventh" chord, which feels somehow unresolved, full of tension, incomplete. But what if that incompleteness is what carries a seed that you are to cherish patiently and with trust? What if the energy in that lack of resolution is what Rilke alludes to in claiming that "the song *remains* beautiful"? That the tensions we feel in what is "unresolved" in our lives are part of this melody? How might accepting this open us to relinquish our need to resolve that tension—in musical terms, to move from the tension of what we feel as a discordant "seventh" chord to what is next?

Composers are the first to remind us that the musical "seventh" is important and not to be avoided. That its discord is what lends music that sense of anticipation of change, leaning toward a resolution even when it is not yet voiced. For the experience of that disharmony is what births our yearning—before we seek to resolve it. Here, the lure of the "octave," at least in western traditions, lends music energy and depth.

Of course, something in us wants to resolve the contradictions we face. To erase the uncertainties and dispel what is unsettling. Rilke refuses this move. And he goes even further to remind us that *we* "are the stillness" between those "two notes." That we are alive between and within these contradictions, not on the other side of them. And that embracing the tensions is what helps us lean forward into change, step by step or *kaizen,* helping us see that we are alive *within* the contradictions of our lives. Because we carry within us the hidden secret of our true self, which is not waiting until we have resolved the tensions. *You are the tree standing before what you once were.*

The journey to live the *questions* that unsettle us is finally just that: letting what is unfinished be what it is: uncertain, incomplete, even disturbing. And, in that incompletion, holding the promise of change. The chance of growth. The hope of transformation. And to embrace those questions even when they seem to us like "a locked room" or "a book written in an utterly unknown language." To let them be because embracing them is what we are given to do—or, more accurately, how we are invited to *be*. At least for now.

Rilke encourages us to let that unresolved chord, that "dark interval" in our lives, be what we "carry" in facing the contradictions. In standing where we *are*. This, at least, is what it means, he tells us, to "live artistically." But this work is not the poet's last word. He does not leave us dangling as if we are abandoned in that darkness. No, he looks ahead of us, knowing that the tensions do come "trembling, to join as one," but only in the dark interval where we learn to embrace what appear to be polarities. To face the contradictions. To affirm the binaries. To seek within these tensions that greater wholeness to which we belong.

As if to underscore this, he does not close the line but leaves it open with the ellipses that follow:

> But in the dark interval both come,
> trembling, to join as one...
>
> > and the song remains beautiful.

The last word is not that the "dark interval" is the whole truth, even though it *is* the one we must face again and again as we make our way in this life. And always in the face of "the note Death." The last word, the decisive truth, the presence in and through all that is—including death—is the "song [that] remains beautiful." Whether or not we recognize it. Whether or not we attend to its melody or miss it in our hurry.

Whether or not we can even hear anything like music given the discordant moment of the "dark interval" in which we find ourselves.

*

Poems like this one remind us that we belong in a dynamic, unresolved world. That "the whole creation has been groaning in travail until now, and not only the creation but we ourselves," as the apostle Paul once put it (Romans 8:22–23). That we belong to a world that is yearning for the wholeness that is somehow already present in the midst of the tensions. At the heart of the uncertainties. And that this is so for each of us as well. This longing arises from an essential "belongingness" that we each carry within us, one that draws us through our desire for relatedness— with our truest, innermost self, and with that of others.

Poems like this one offer glimpses of what would otherwise remain hidden to us, speaking quietly if often unheard in the depths of the soul. They resist that what Keats called "negative capability," that "irritable reaching after fact and reason" which closes us to mystery and takes from us the courage to live the questions.

Such poems encourage us to break down our resistances to inner kindness, compassion, and understanding. Because the voice of strong poems like this one gesture from the "innerness" of the poet's own being to that which he shares with us all—and which we share with one another, most poignantly at the places of our uncertainties, anxieties, and doubts. Such poems lean toward true communion by welcoming us to embrace a wider and more generous belonging. *I am the stillness. You are the stillness. We are the stillness.*

*

I invite you to receive the following words as if Rilke had written them directly for *you*, as if you received them in a time of confusion and uncertainty in your life:

Don't search now for answers that can't be given to you, because you can't live them. And it finally comes down to this: to live everything. *Live* the questions now. Perhaps on some distant day you'll find yourself, slowly and unknowingly, living into the answer. Perhaps you already carry within yourself the possibility to create and shape—as a particularly sacred and pure way of living. Raise yourself in such a way. But take what comes with great trust, and even if it seems to come through an act of will, from some inner compulsion, take it upon yourself and do not despise it.

Rilke urges you to take heed of the power you carry within yourself, describing it as "the possibility to create and shape." Not to create something, but *to create the work of art that you are.* And do it as a path of living, as a way of being, as a means of belonging.

Breathe in the stillness that you are, finding in this a source of wonder alongside the inevitable limitations and uncertainties you face. Begin by discovering that *you are the stillness,* and in that discovery sense how it feels to ground yourself where you stand, to be *"the tree that stands before what [you] once were."* Live into the stillness you *are,* deep in your "innerness," amid the tensions that are unresolved—and perhaps unresolvable—in your life.

Begin with your questions. Let them become portals, flung wide open. You are not a project that needs to be completed, but at every stage of your life a being on the way toward greater wholeness. This is not the mark of imperfection. It is the occasion of curiosity and discovery, of opening and growth. It is the heart of your own deepest and truest creativity.

Try opening yourself to the discoveries that are closest to hand, that lead you step by step—*kaizen*—along the path of discovering the uniqueness of your life. That you are part of the song that sings its way through you, and through all that is. And that your work is to be faithful to the truth that, come what may, "the song remains…beautiful."

CHAPTER 9

WHERE DO I BELONG?

Whoever you are: when evening comes, go out
of your familiar room where you know everything;
for your house stands on the edge of distances—
whoever you are.
With your eyes, so tired they can barely
free themselves from the worn threshold,
lift with measured pace a single, black tree
and place it before the skies: slender and alone.
And you have made the world. And it is vast
and like a word still ripening in the silences.
And just as your will grasps its meaning,
your eyes let it tenderly go...

—"Entrance"

[*STEPHANIE DOWRICK*]

"Whoever you are" is surely one of the most inviting opening phrases of
any poem, with an inescapable resonance for this time, for *our* time. In
a mere three words it creates a sweep that gathers us all up and in, not
into any predictable sameness but into our glorious diversity, *whoever we
are*. No one is left out. In a time when suffocating conformity is too often
demanded of us, even while cheapened notions of individual freedoms and
"freedom of thought" are cynically paraded, an invitation to belong uncon-
ditionally to yourself and to life, *whoever you are*, is wondrously radical.

Belonging evokes safety, presence: a chance to breathe out and "let go." It says *Yes*, whoever you are. And while unconditional belonging—"Home is the place where they have to take you in"—is the most precious of all, for many in our world it is no more than a dream.

*

This is where lived experience is, as always, our best teacher. Each of us knows deep in our bones how bruising even a mild experience of exclusion can be. To be viewed through a self-righteous, hostile gaze is searing. To be driven out, scorned, humiliated is devastating. Indeed, a fear of abandonment lives deep in our bones and can dominate the psyche.

Yet, as I write this, even mild deviations from conformity are still being punished in so-called advanced societies through shaming, shunning, and even exiling some from *the one human family to which we all belong.* As seriously, many people see others only through the prism of their own most immediate needs. "When you don't meet my needs any longer, I will walk away and dump you." This turns complex human beings into commodities, at least in others' experiencing of them. It is immature; it is inhumane. It is also dangerous. To have to fight for relational stability, consideration, inclusion, or respect, whatever your age, demands huge resilience. And resilience is finite in most of us.

Rilke's own childhood may have led him to write, as an adult, "There are no classes in life for beginners: right away you are always asked to deal with what is most difficult." Add in structural issues of race, social class, gender, sexuality, or disability, and what an individual is asked to bear may be far too much to bear. It may feel and be unendurable. All but the most strenuously defended will feel diminished by the bleak judgments of others telling us *we don't belong,* we don't fit in, we are not what's wanted. Or even allowed.

Some of the saddest examples of this come when fundamentalists, within religious communities or faith groups, take it upon themselves to judge who will be "saved" or condemned—for "all eternity." And, in this life, who will be valued and cherished, and who will be feared, despised, perhaps even banished. It's the shadow of religious mania at its worst. Global examples of "not belonging" are driven by bigotry based on race, skin color, and other outward identifiers, and these stereotypes spread fear, suspicion, cruelty, exploitation, and violence throughout our world.

Such ugliness of perspective denies the truth of our human condition. It denies our human potential, even in those who believe themselves to be privileged. Spiritual truths are much simpler. As the ancient Buddhist *metta* meditation puts it: *May all beings be well and happy. May all beings be free from harm. May all beings live in peace.* Our happiness and our survival depend on appreciating and responding to our common needs, our interbeing and relatedness.

*

Indeed, an alert sense of relatedness, with interest and respect, is basic to any understanding of belonging. It is also a spiritual imperative more important than any other. The apostle Paul expressed it strongly in a famous letter to early followers of Christ: "If I have the gift of prophecy and can fathom all mysteries and all knowledge, and if I have a faith that can move mountains, but have not love, I am nothing. If I give all I possess to the poor and surrender my body to the flames, but have not love, I gain nothing" (1 Corinthians 13:1).

In the exquisite older Hindu scripture, the *Bhagavad Gita* (Song of the Lord), the Lord Krishna assures the young prince Arjuna—and all who would later hear or read this, that "All states of being begin in me. They are *in* me, not I in them…I am with all beings always; I abandon no one. However great your sorrows, you are never separated from me." As though those riches of visionary relatedness and belonging were not enough, the 17th-century religious poet Angelus Silesius added that "Love can certainly be difficult. Because to love is not enough. We must, like God, become love."

Don't quail! *Whoever you are*, you are unlikely to have the power to change others' behaviors or even to influence their attitudes more positively, necessarily. Where you do have power and agency is to grow your willingness to support others in *their* belonging—which may be another way of showing love. In every area of your life there will be opportunities to include others more actively in your considerations: to give to others a sense of inclusion and the respect that comes with it, to listen to the voices routinely excluded in your community or nation, to look deeply at some of your own assumptions—*your familiar room where you know everything*.

The *yes* or *no* or *maybe* of belonging can be a ceaseless dance present in every encounter. It is there when a young Indigenous man is followed around a shop while his non-Indigenous mates are left alone to browse. It is there when someone loses a chance for a job interview or promotion because their first name is Mohammed. Or Mehreen. It is there driving the Black Lives Matter movement in the United States and across the world. It is vivid in the life of every "trans" person. And continues in the lives of many gay people, too.

There are also the many, many people who, without diagnosis or definition, just know themselves to be "different." This may bring a pain-filled inner loneliness when there is no group or tribe with which they—or you—can readily affiliate. Perhaps then there is no *familiar room where you know everything*. Not now, not anywhere. When someone no longer fits in with the demands of their old "belonging," or when they are shunned or exiled, this also produces a level of loneliness that can be harrowing and even life-threatening.

You may find clues through deep listening to others, and patient, compassionate listening to yourself. You may help yourself also when you can *give* the precious experience of belonging to others, perhaps through conscious gestures of inclusion, thoughtfulness, kindness, deep listening, consideration of their reality, especially when you long for a greater sense of belonging for your own self.

> With your eyes, so tired they can barely
> free themselves from the worn threshold,
> lift with measured pace a single, black tree
> and place it before the skies: slender and alone.
> And you have made the world.

*

Belonging—and yearning to belong—stirs something deep within us. It feels like an experience of soul. But it's also physiological. As infants, we will not survive without the care that comes with belonging. This must nurture us emotionally as well as physically if we are to flourish. Or even survive. Only as we grow and individuate does our "belonging" become more complex. In the process we might also come to know that there are structural hierarchies within our societies that will challenge and disrupt our primary needs—or those of others.

My husband Paul is a pediatrician who has lived in Australia's Northern Territory and worked in remote First Nations communities in Australia for more than 40 years. Paul tells me with sorrow that many of his young patients, who have more than their share of life-shortening illnesses due to poverty and endemic racism, will mostly be as full of life as any child until they are about eight. Then society's attitudes, delivered on drip-feed through television, internet, and other media, will teach them how different their lives are from those they view and absorb daily.

Questions of belonging loom large in this example. First Nations children in Australia belong to the oldest living cultures in the world. They can trace the lineage of their many clans and nations back 65,000 years. Yet, when Captain Cook and Joseph Banks "discovered" Australia in 1770, they declared it *terra nullius*, "no one's land," justifying the British invasion and possession with the claim that this ancient continent "belonged" to no one.

*

In one of Sufi poet Rumi's poems from the 13th century he calls out, "Come, come whoever you are, / wanderer, worshipper, lover of leaving. / It doesn't matter. / Ours is not a caravan of despair. /…Though you have broken your vows a thousand times, / come…." I have spoken, chanted, or sung these words so many times in my spiritual teaching. They enclose everyone. They leave no one out. They speak of hope and new chances. *Ours is not a caravan of despair.* That for me is the only measure of authentic spirituality.

Whether our own story of belonging/not belonging is large-scale or subtle, we will likely also discover that belonging is not a once-and-for-ever experience. This is vivid when it comes to claiming our own values, our place in the world, where we sense ourselves fitting in, or where "fitting in" is not right for us.

Belonging fluctuates even within our own sense of self: "To thine own self be true." It may take several experiences of wondering, *who am I?* as a jolting experience of not quite "belonging" to wake us up to our own inner contradictions as well as our emerging potentials. *Living into your questions* is very real in this context. It's a potent reminder that no part of you is static; inner and outer change, with all the uncertainties, is inevitable and not to be feared or thwarted.

Profound questions around gender or sexuality may fracture a sense of inner as well as outer belonging. Geographical, as well as psychic or emotional displacement, stirs up questions around belonging that those who remain "local" through a lifetime may never encounter. On many levels, Rilke's life illustrates that. He was born in 1875 into a German-speaking family in Czech-speaking Prague, then capital of the Austrian province of Bohemia. He was a male child born to a grieving mother who would have preferred her recently deceased infant daughter to be replaced by another girl. René—as his parents originally named him—was sent as a young boy to a military school to toughen him up, which he was constitutionally unable to do.

Years later, as a young man still finding his way in early adulthood, he married the sculptor Clara Westhoff and had a child whom they named Ruth, yet we know from his letters and journals that he remained far more attached to his former lover, the writer and psychoanalyst Lou Andreas-Salomé. It is worth noting, too, that while Rilke wrote stir-ringly about intimacy, a carefully guarded solitude was almost always his preferred state. His cultivated identity as a "poet" was a constant, even through times when he believed the heights of inspiration were inaccessible to him. "Poet" was the sum of his inwardness that he protected above all else.

On the more external issue of a *national identity* as key to belonging, Rilke was unequivocal. He thought of himself as "European," not "Austrian" or "Bohemian" and certainly not "German." His instincts were always opposed to nationalism and the powerfully destructive fervor that can drive it. He lived in defiance of any form of narrowing the mind. At a time when there was no common parlance to express this, his interest was in freeing his own vision and widening his consciousness. Not boundaries, with their often-dangerous limitations, but "the Open" was his way of identifying his place within the world. In doing that, he frees ours.

None of his unconventional choices need take away from our enjoyment of reading Rilke. On the contrary. Those very complexities highlight what brings him closest to us, illuminating our own maturing and unfolding self-understanding. Among the deepest questions many live with are those that relate to identity, conformity, acceptance by others, perhaps on their terms, through their own learnings or leanings. Nationalism is a primal call, a version of tribalism that also extends to sub-groups, whether political, religious, or cultural. It is, in turn, manipulated by those who harness it to secure or extend their power, offering a sense of belonging that too often depends upon crude "othering," binary thinking that divides "us" from "them."

Perhaps only someone who has had many *felt* experiences of not-belonging, who knows that despite "the familiar room where you know everything" their "house stands on the edge of distances," will comprehend how laden this experience is. Yet—and I welcome this paradox—shedding the certainties that belonging may demand can simultaneously be freeing or enlightening. A slow inner-directed re-reading of this poem may be best, to intuit how these words are *yours*, as well as Rilke's:

> Whoever you are: when evening comes, go out
> of your familiar room where you know everything;

for your house stands on the edge of distances—
whoever you are.
With your eyes, so tired they can barely
free themselves from the worn threshold,
lift with measured pace a single, black tree
and place it before the skies: slender and alone.
And you have made the world. And it is vast
and like a word still ripening in the silences.
And just as your will grasps its meaning,
your eyes let it tenderly go...

Belonging *and* not belonging are human experiences. That means they are subject to outer influences as well as inner conditioning.

I have lived independently, if at times chaotically and recklessly, from an early age. Because I had no trusted inner anchor in my younger life, I made my own way relying on that early love of reading, learning, thinking for myself which both my parents—but especially my mother—gave me. What I also had was an instinct for meaning: that life is precious and to make something of it was the only way I could learn to recognize myself. That "something" had to be more than a job and a wage; that idealism, too, was my fortunate inheritance. Writing, oddly, has offered me both inner restlessness and belonging. Do I love it then? Only sometimes. Am I compelled to do it? Rilke speaks for me when he wrote, "Ask yourself, in the most silent hour of the night, *must I write?*"

*

This short, intense poem, "Entrance," offers an experience of transformation, of *inner* hospitality, of wholeness elevating belonging. Its very title speaks of beginnings, thresholds, taking that first step or first deep conscious breath of the day. The poem acknowledges our strangeness, how we can feel like a stranger to ourselves sometimes, even as the poem—and the poet—urge us to belong fully to the unique gift of life that is ours, one that we share with every other living being. This sense of interbeing is true independence, one that grounds us in our own lives while simultaneously connecting us to what Rilke often referred to simply as "the Whole."

This is his remarkable genius. This is an insight to absorb and treasure. Indeed, I'd go so far as to say that this insight centers and guides my spiritual life. That driving sense of coherence—*whoever you are*—takes in all that we are. It takes in *all* that *you* are. Let Rilke's words again be yours for a moment, ideally saying them aloud, feeling them emerge from your own mouth, shifting the breath within you and the air around you. I will translate them into first person for this purpose:

> *Whoever I am: when evening comes, [I may] leave*
> *my familiar room where I know everything;*
> *for my house stands on the edge of distances—*
> *whoever I am.*

Can you feel something of the steadiness of Rilke's promise, along with his truthful acknowledgment of life's precariousness? This is truly *a question to live into*. It is what art itself reaches for, and what it seeks to make manifest. Let Rilke's voice speak again now:

> With your eyes, so tired they can barely
> free themselves from the worn threshold,
> lift with measured pace a single, black tree
> and place it before the skies: slender and alone.
> And you have made the world. And it is vast
> and like a word still ripening in the silences.
> And just as your will grasps its meaning,
> your eyes let it tenderly go...

Where is that *single black tree*—that stark reminder that *life goes on*—in your inner landscape? A genuine poet's job is to wonder and provoke, not to soothe. That's solely the business of Hallmark cards. We are, after all, living with change, inevitably. Inner change and outer. We grow;

we grow older. We grow in health; we decline in health. We grow in wisdom; we rediscover foolishness. We grow in strength; we fail in our fragility. We breathe and, eventually, cease breathing.

Courage is needed to comprehend these basic facts. We are mortal beings, moving at every moment from birth towards an inevitable bodily death. What's more, such courage must be gathered up not as an abstraction but in the present tense. *This* moment. Not knowing "everything" is already taking you from the "house," from that "familiar room where you know everything," from the security and reassurance of your best-known self, to the "edge of distances."

Rilke seems to affirm two states of mind simultaneously. That's familiar when we say, "I'm in two minds about…" Here, it's a longing to go forward, risking unchartered distances, and, equally, a longing to hold back. You've perhaps been in this place of ambivalence many times. Rilke repeats the phrase that includes and perhaps recognizes you: *whoever you are.*

> *Whoever you are*: when evening comes, go out
> of your familiar room where you know everything;
> for your house stands on the edge of distances—
> *whoever you are* [my italics].

When Rilke warns that *"your house stands on the edge of distances,* he reminds us that the known is neighbor-close to the unknown, however obsessively or anxiously we plan. Things happen. Things change. And will again. Our desire for control, for certainty, must sometimes be surrendered, *whoever you are.* How prepared for that are you?

Rilke comes closer still. He acknowledges your weariness. He calls you to go beyond it. He writes, with a tenderness born from lived experience:

> …With your eyes, so tired they can barely
> free themselves from the worn threshold…

Our eyes *are* tired. You and I must witness so much in our world—and often enough in our own lives—that is harsh, idiotic, unjust, divisive, unacceptable. Anything but wholesome. How could you be anything but exhausted? And the threshold? Not merely a known place of leaving and returning, but also *worn* by those crossings.

Threshold is a word I relish. It was often used by the late Irish poet and philosopher John O'Donohue. I can't read the word without hearing it spoken in his gorgeous Connemara accent, where every word becomes a musical note, and a poem becomes a song. *Threshold* is something we cross many times a day, consciously and unconsciously, both the physical and metaphorical or spiritual kinds, the latter taking us from one state of mind or awareness to another.

When we are bone-tired aren't we more likely to cling to the known? Or to huddle within the familiar when we are afraid, even when doing so may well harm us? Habits are compelling. Stepping out takes courage. It takes energy that we may not believe we have. Ah…but now it is creativity—that vast resource we know as the human imagination—that comes to our rescue:

> With your eyes, so tired they can barely
> free themselves from the worn threshold,
> lift with measured pace a single, black tree
> and place it before the skies: slender and alone.
> And you have made the world. And it is vast
> and like a word still ripening in the silences.
> And just as your will grasps its meaning,
> your eyes let it tenderly go…

To lift with measured pace *a single, black tree / and place it before the skies: slender and alone*, is a mighty act. It is an act of consciousness as well as creativity. It is choice. It is choosing.

Don't over-think this image of *a single black tree…single and alone*. Conjure it in your own way. Let it bring something freeing to you. Let it for a moment belong to and be within you. For with this simple, extraordinary act, this sacred communing between you and yourself, you and nature, Rilke tells you that "*you have made the world. And it is vast / and like a word still ripening in the silences.* And then, perhaps unexpectedly, it happens:

> And just as your will grasps its meaning,
> your eyes let it tenderly go...

*

In another poem, Rilke reminds us that *nothing belongs to us.* Is *that* paradox bearable? Is the truth also bearable that we "belong" to life, to ourselves and to others? That it is neither solitude nor intimacy that guarantees belonging, but *both* deepening our inviolable capacity for relatedness?

I hope so.

Because the truth of our longing and need to belong does co-exist with multiple acts of *letting go.* This is painfully, agonizingly difficult when we haven't had—have not yet received into ourselves—whatever is most meaningful for this existence. Letting go may be bearable—sometimes "just bearable"—when you can welcome the senses, experiences, and emotions that you yearn for. And trust them in their partialness and imperfection. Belong into them and they into you. Then, you have made the world.

In one of his posthumously published *Letters to a Young Poet*, Rilke wrote to Franz Kappus that

> ...we have no reason to mistrust our world, for it is not against us. Has it terrors, they are our terrors; has its abysses, they belong to us; are dangers at hand, we must try to love them... How should we be able to forget those ancient myths about dragons that at any moment turn into princesses? Perhaps all the dragons of our lives are princesses who are only waiting to see us once beautiful and brave.

The world, after all, is *still ripening in the silences.*

In the silences, you may be readiest to surrender to *being*...and to belonging. The world we make is vast. And ripening. Each of us belongs. *Each of us belongs.*

CHAPTER 10

DELIGHTING IN YOUR BODY

Wait . . ., that's delicious . . . Already it's on the run.
. . . . Just a bit of music, a stamping, a hum –:
girls, you who're warm, girls, you who're mute,
dance the savor of the fruit you've tasted!

Dance the orange. Who can forget this,
how, drowning in itself, it defends itself
against its own sweetness. You've possessed it.
It has converted itself deliciously toward you.

Dance the orange. The warmer landscape,
throw it forth from within you so that the ripe orange might
    shine
in your homeland's winds! You that glowed, unveil

fragrance upon fragrance. Establish kinship
with the pure, resisting rind,
with the juice that fills the happy fruit!

— *The Sonnets to Orpheus* I.15

[*MARK S. BURROWS*]

When I first read this poem, years ago, my immediate response was one
of sheer delight—which is what the poem is all about. It's a strange,

wonderful sensation, one that children experience with simple immediacy: tasting the sweetness of a juicy orange for the first time or watching a kite dart here and there in the morning winds; seeing a butterfly flitting from flower to flower or noticing the changing shape of a billowy cloud. It still can be so for us, of course, which is the sense of this sonnet.

And yes, this is a poem about sensing, about opening ourselves to the beauty of which we are a part and experiencing it as it presents itself to us—to be savored in and through our body's senses, with attentiveness and gratitude. About being alive in our bodies and finding delight in and through them—to the point of delighting *in* our bodies. This is a poem about presence, real presence: the world's *and our own* as we discover ourselves as belonging to it, as part of what Rilke calls "the Whole."

"Wait..., that's delicious": what a strange way to open a poem. It seems an interruption, as if the poet found himself in the middle of a tedious task when he suddenly experienced something that startled him with delight—and, just as suddenly, it was gone again. The experience of delight is like this. It might come upon us suddenly, like the first time we tasted something utterly delicious, only to find that it was over altogether too soon: "Already it's on the run."

Such fleeting moments of joy startle us. They awaken us to the world. They invite us to be alive in our bodies, to be awake to the particularities of this embodied life. They remind us, amid the pain and suffering we face, that we are made for delight—a truth we often fail to remember. How does this awareness come to us? It could be anything: "just a bit of music, a stamping, a hum," and we're ready to dance.

Or are we? Are you? Perhaps you are feeling a bit cautious at this point. *Me? Ready to dance? I don't think so.* After all, there are at least a hundred reasons why this does not seem possible. Or desirable. Or even appropriate. *What will they think of me? How can I dare to let myself go in the flow of all this? Can I even imagine entering the dance? Do I deserve to take a chance on delight?*

Such notes of caution, of course, are not your problem alone. We live in a world flooded with enticements toward unreachable things, saturated with self-defeating images—of a kind of body-perfection that is unattainable, and even unimaginable, for most of us. Images that deflate us in the endless downward spiral of comparisons to others and *their* beauty, real or surmised.

And then we come upon those opening words of the poem, "Wait a moment...," and see Rilke himself pausing, as if interrupted from something else he'd been doing when he suddenly found himself opened wide to what was present to him. And a few abbreviated lines later, we hear his ridiculous—and ridiculously wonderful—call to "dance the orange." More on that in a moment.

Let us first consider the abruptness of the poem's opening lines, which come as a sudden and unexpected outburst. Like the moment when you find yourself startled by something utterly delightful. There is an immediacy here. No second-guessing. No hesitating or qualifying; no ignoring or evading. What Rilke describes is the kind of enthusiasm we experienced as children, and sometimes still do as adults, when we encounter something for the first time that enchants us. And then we remember something we are prone to forget: namely, that delight is an emotion we are made for.

It's also a way of experiencing beauty within the aliveness of our bodies, a subversive way that sees it not as some kind of rarified quality of perfection that is outside of or utterly beyond us. No, it is the experience of seeing beauty as something that happens *to* us, that lies *within* our experience—in this case, by opening ourselves to what is delightful. The moment of *being* that beauty because we *are*, and not because of what we might become. And yes: it has to do with our remembering that *we are delightable*. That you and I can delight *in* and *through* the precious body that is like a "temple" of the spirit.

*

In the first of his *Letters to a Young Poet*, Rilke wrote to his young correspondent to encourage him to shift his focus as a writer and open himself to his own creativity. Rilke advised the young poet to set aside evaluations of his competence or talent as a poet and to embrace the sources of life arising within him. He counseled the aspiring writer to "go inside yourself."

This seems obvious, but it is utterly necessary to shape one's life creatively: *Go inside yourself.* Seek the pulse of your heart. Find the source of your delight—or fear. Don't compare yourself to others. Don't reduce yourself to wishful thinking: *If only...if only...if only...I were...*

Remember, too, that no one else can do this for you; you must lead this expedition yourself. Or, better: you must discover yourself as an explorer—of your own life. You must decide what *you* must do—and what you *must* do—to live creatively. Don't think about it; don't make plans for it as for a future endeavor. "Build your life according to this necessity," Rilke goes on to say. Seize the moment. Do it *now.*

Such advice sounds true but stands against a relentless tide in cultures like ours, based on unattainable images of what it is we might possibly desire. And influenced by their shadowed sibling, deferral. *Not now. Not yet. Not me.* We live in a society that seems obsessed with planning for some hoped-for future, or an unreachable desire, both of which turn us from the one moment we have—which is *here* and *now.* Of course, in many dimensions of our lives, this might be entirely sensible. But not in terms of our creative, responsive, intuitive, *original* life. "Dance the taste of the experienced fruit!"

Rilke here reminds us to take what is close at hand and...dance it. When you read these words, what comes to mind? Can you imagine heeding such an invitation? And what would it look like, this image of "dancing" what you have already experienced—whether fruit, or weather, or a snatch of birdsong overheard from some unseen place above you in the trees? Or the wondrous gift that is your very life?

What would it mean to take that experience and "dance" it? And to do so not with some complicated form, but perhaps with something as simple as letting your hand move freely in the air as if you were directing musicians awaiting your guidance as they prepare to bring forth music from the silences? Or even imagining, in your mind, moving gracefully across the stage, and in that imagining—as you stand quietly, your eyes closed, your body motionless—you begin to feel your body flowing with newfound joy?

Here, the only tense that matters is the present. *Tomorrow* is an abstraction; being present to your creativity *now* is what counts. "If your everyday life seems poor to you," Rilke continues in that letter, "don't blame it. Blame yourself that you aren't poet enough to call forth its riches"—as he knows you *can*.

*

Rilke is not chiding his young counterpart for being inadequate here. He is inviting him—and you, with him—to discover the innate capacity to create, to enrich life by opening to its presence, to delights already experienced as well as those that await, here and now. How might you become "poet enough" to be this receptive, this creative, in your harried, busy, or sometimes painfully empty life? There are no rigid or set formulae here. No absolute, sure-fire recipes. Just a call to surrender to newly spacious *seeing* and *being*—and yes, perhaps even to *dancing*.

Open yourself to the interruptions—which, as one wise writer suggested, are the moments when grace happens. Seize what is ordinary and open yourself to it. Like the scent of balsam pine deep in the woods on a crisp winter's morning, or the touch of a dear friend's hand in a painful season of grief. Like the sound of a stream coursing gently downward toward the sea, or a gentle laugh shared with someone you love. Like the chorus of birds in that quiet hour just before sunrise when the world—and you yourself—are still enough that you can hear it, or a moment when you remember an image of happiness from some time in your past. Like the relief you can almost taste when rain falls on parched ground after a long dry spell, or the satisfaction of cows sitting as they chew their cud quietly beneath a shade tree that shelters them from the afternoon sun. "Dance the taste of the experienced fruit!"

*

As Rilke elsewhere reminds us, "Most people don't have any idea how beautiful the world is and how much radiance reveals itself in the smallest of things." Most people, perhaps, but what of you? Are you poet enough to open yourself to this radiance in any one of its myriad expressions? "Wait...that's delicious..."

A sceptic might complain that Rilke is voicing wishful thinking. That he is a naïve optimist. Perhaps, though the world of beauty—which is always available to us, despite the horrors—remains what it is for those with eyes to see. The only question is: *Do you have such eyes?* Are you ready for this surprise? Will you open yourself to discover it beneath its outward disguise? Will you remember this, knowing that you carry the capacity to delight within yourself? That the temple of your body somehow knows that *you are the future?*

Children remind us of this when we had forgotten, showing us how the world offers itself to the imagination. This is surely why we delight in their presence as we grow older. They reveal to us something we always carry in our "innerness": the capacity to enjoy the moment, to "seize the day," as the adage puts it. In my own life, the gift of my two daughters became a primary invitation for me to heed this call and risk dancing—the orange or anything else readily at hand. Their instinctive openness to joy, their capacity to seize the world about them, their unbridled delight in discovering "radiance reveal[ing] itself in the smallest of things" often beckoned me to turn from work, with all its importance, to the essential call of play.

I learned from them that what mattered most was always already here. Always already now. That everything depended on whether I noticed it, and that in turn depended on how I opened myself to such noticing. What matters most, I discovered with them, was the work of *becoming poet enough* to embrace the beauty that is always waiting, often amid everything that seems opposed to it: those "uncertainties, Mysteries, and doubts" Keats reminded us of, as well as those nagging fears and anxieties we carry like unwanted baggage through life.

This is what Jesus described as "the kingdom of heaven" which he compared to a merchant seeking beautiful treasures who, "when he had found one pearl of great price, went and sold all that he had and bought it" (Matthew 13:45–46). And while it may be true in this parable that the first task is to find that pearl, the second is just as important: to make the sacrifice necessary to open ourselves to acquire it in our lives. This is not strategic planning, not outcome-based learning; it is poetry. Jesus speaks here not as an investment manager or financial advisor. He addresses us as a poet. Look for this pearl in the "radiance that reveals itself in the smallest of things." Do it *now*.

*

When reading a poem that begins, as this one does, with an outburst of joy, we can only surmise what had occupied the poet before this moment happened. We know it, though, in our own lives: the press of things-to-do. But even now I can overhear my then six-year-old daughter inviting me to turn aside from the burden of work to discover little bursts of this playful radiance with her—"in the smallest of things." For me, such moments remind me of the call to become "poet enough" to open myself to wonder. To relinquish my strong sense of seriousness to find, again, my inner child. To remain open to astonishment, to one's freshest senses, remains a challenge for me, but one that is oh so well worth pursuing.

What of you? Do you long for such moments in your life? Do you yearn to find yourself suddenly lifted by the gentle hand of gladness? To be startled into unexpected delight? To be surprised by some experience that rises up within you and through you like a gusher of joy? Can you find yourself, as you read this opening line, being lured by some interrupting glimpse of radiance?

In an important sense, your very life depends on this. This is not an option to be exercised in times of leisure—or not only in such moments. Rilke's opening line suggests the urgency he felt in writing, and the immediacy he hoped to convey to you who are reading this poem. It's as if he wants you to join him as he bites into a juicy orange, and in a moment of exuberance to shout out with him in delight: *"Wait…, that's delicious!"*

This is, of course, a moment, and one that cannot necessarily be sustained. *"Already it's on the run,"* he goes on to write. What remains, though, is the reminder you carry within yourself as you journey back into the tedious hours, a memory that lights a flame deep in your heart as you turn to whatever creases of darkness present themselves. For even a glimpse of radiance lingers, and in that lingering continues to awaken something essential within you.

In this strange opening line Rilke catches a glorious moment of deliciousness that had startled him—and then was gone. This, too, he knew, was true of beauty, since it is an experience that you must come to discover concretely, at the heart of your finitude. It *happens* to you, in and through the instrument that is your body.

As the American philosopher Frederick Turner puts it, "a beautiful thing, though simple in its immediate presence, always gives us a sense of depth below depth, almost an innocent wild vertigo as one falls through its levels." If it is true to say we "fall in love," perhaps we might also say we can "fall in delight." That we "fall in beauty," at least if we are "poet enough" to seize it here and now, with all the imperfections.

*

This poem may seem to you on first reading as foolish, or extravagant. In a certain sense, of course, it is both. This is precisely Rilke's point. It also beckons us to that "sense of depth below depth," in and through the finite things of experience. Through all this, he sensed in his time—as we do in ours—a malaise that the pressures of late-modern capitalism have brought upon us: namely, a realization that our minds are "governed by the calculus of consumerism and busyness," as John O'Donohue put it, so that "we are less and less frequently available to the exuberance of beauty."

Too often, we accept versions of "beauty" that merely point to an unrealizable or even manufactured version of perfection—with photoshopped images of exquisitely sculpted bodies and other artificially enhanced portraits. These set most of us up for disappointment of various sorts, often throwing us into the downward spiral of humiliation, frustration, and shame. Often to the point of depression.

Yet O'Donohue reminds us that "the hidden heart of beauty offers itself only when it is approached in a rhythm worthy of its trust and showing." What is this rhythm? It is the pulse that supports you in discovering *your* inner or original beauty, a deep radiance within you that discloses your true self in a culture too easily infatuated with the artificial and superficial. And this is what makes you, whoever you are, "poet enough" to "dance the orange."

Rilke calls us to delight in glimpses of radiance, to *taste* beauty—and he means this quite literally, since he is remembering the experience of biting into a juicy orange, its juices spilling forth as the fruit "converted itself deliciously toward you." The image makes me smile as I imagine this poet—always impeccably dressed in a starched white shirt, slender tie and neatly ironed suit, polished shoes often with spats—sharing the experience with these girls of biting into a juicy orange and then calling them all to "dance the savor of the fruit you've tasted!"

The poem is a testimonial to the body's powers to experience delight in the ways we "taste" the world. It is a paean to sensuality, in this case pointing to the tongue's way of thrilling us in finding what is here for us to enjoy. Rilke felt no reluctance in celebrating the body, remaining far closer to the apostle Paul's conviction that the body is "the temple of the sacred spirit" than to later puritanical prohibitions that refused most forms of delight—and above all *dance*.

Over the years I have spent delighting in this poem, I've come to hear echoes of the great American poet Walt Whitman in his insistence that "the fruition of beauty is no chance of hit or miss...it is inevitable as life... it is exact and plumb as gravitation." Indeed, he opens his exuberant, anti-puritanical creed, *Leaves of Grass*, with a joyful outburst, declaring that "I celebrate myself," and goes on to voice his personal creed:

> I believe in the flesh and the appetites,
> Seeing, hearing and feeling are miracles, and each part

and tag of me is a miracle.
Divine am I inside and out, and I make holy whatever
I touch or am touched from;
The scent of these armpits is aroma finer than prayer,
This head is more than churches or bibles or creeds.
If I worship any particular thing it shall be some of
the spread of my body...
...I dote on myself.... there is that lot of me, and all so luscious.
Each moment and whatever happens thrills me with joy.

This is ecstatic experience. This is an outburst of exuberant delight, occasioned by the most ordinary of physical moments. This is a celebration of the embodied spirit by the writer who once described himself as "the poet of the body...[and] the poet of the soul." This is the creed of an exultant voice who was offended by—and offended—the narrow moralists of his day, just as Rilke's sonnet might have done and might still do to the puritans among us, whose warnings we often cower at and sometimes succumb to.

Rilke joins Whitman in decrying the restrictive codes of behavior that refuse delight. That exclude celebrating the body as the "temple" of joy. That cannot imagine affirming "how much radiance reveals itself in the smallest of things." In and through our bodies as the sacred gateways by which we experience the world. Here Rilke, like Whitman, was not trying to scandalize. He joins his predecessor in having no interest simply in shocking—though this surely could be the poem's effect.

No, his intent is to unsettle us, to startle us into experiencing ourselves, in our bodies, as the vital portal of the true self. He is reminding us that our body is not an *object* to be desired; it is a desiring *subject*. It is the way you and I experience the world, the intimate means by which we build our sense of who we are. And, yes, the vehicle in which we learn to "dance" this world.

Since he knows how high the stakes are, Rilke's address in this sonnet is unhesitating and direct. For we could ignore all this and live according to the sterile laws of management, diminishing ourselves by the dictates of a cold rationality driven by the need to control. Exuberance is the key he writes in, gathering his poetic melody from his body's experience:

> Dance the orange. The warmer landscape,
> throw it forth from within you so that the ripe orange might
>   shine
> in your homeland's winds!

In another of Rilke's *Sonnets to Orpheus*, this one written perhaps a day earlier, he writes of experiencing the deliciousness of fruit—the "full-ness" of an apple, banana, pear, and—unexpectedly—the tart tang of gooseberries, and then suggests how we might remember this:

> Read it on a child's face
>
> when it tastes them. This comes from afar.
> Is it being slowly rendered nameless in your mouth?
> Where words once were discoveries now flow,
> startled in being freed from the fruit's flesh. [I.13]

Here, Rilke sees a child's experience embodying something essential to us as human beings: the ability to experience life directly, creatively, and immediately, in and through the body. A step away from the mediation of language back into a primary, original experience.

In the delicious moment captured in this poem, he helps us see that our adult habit of falling back on words or ideas can betray us, turning us from the directness of our body's experience. This seems to lie behind Jesus' insistence, against the sober judgment of his followers, to "let the children come" to him, "for it is to such as these that the kingdom of heaven belongs" (Matthew 19. 14).

The chances are that if you called others to heed Rilke's bold command, they might quietly wonder if you'd lost your sanity. After all, Rilke's admonition—and it comes as a command, not as a tentative invitation—*is* far-fetched. Even ridiculous. "Dance the orange"? Seriously? Yes, this is a playful admonition, but precisely such play *is* serious. Whatever Jesus meant by referring to "the kingdom of heaven"—and biblical scholars still debate this point—he was gesturing toward the extravagant embrace of beauty in its most startling yet enduring forms.

*

In *Ten Windows*, an insightful poet of our day, Jane Hirshfield, points to "surprise" in suggesting what makes strong poems work as they do. In startling us, she writes, such poems change us by "transport[ing] us into previously unanticipatable comprehensions." Rilke's command to "dance the orange" is an instance of this, the heart of a poem that beckons us into what Hirshfield calls "strongly shifted knowledge" from what we normally draw on to govern our lives.

Yet it is precisely such knowing that's what we need to thrive. Perhaps even to discover, as children do, that the "kingdom of heaven" is not to be found in some transcendent "there" and "then," but *here and now*, in your life and mine.

I realize, of course, that in reading this book you've made a decision to open yourself to Rilke's mentoring, or to explore accepting him as a guide for your "heartwork." You may be choosing, consciously or unconsciously, not only to "live the questions" rather than worrying about finding the right answers, but also to open yourself to *poetry* as a portal of self-discovery.

It may be, though, that you might be thinking to yourself, *Well, Rilke—or Burrows—writes as a poet, and poets can imagine anything, even something as ridiculous as this. But that's beyond me.* Somewhere in the back of your mind, you might even recall the Queen in Lewis Carroll's *Alice in Wonderland* who admitted, with unconcealed pride, that she "sometimes...believed as many as six impossible things before breakfast." *She* might have agreed to "dance the orange" but what about *you?* If you enter this dance, can you imagine letting yourself go without worrying about what others are thinking? Could you risk a joy that edges into ecstasy? Could you dance—if only in your imagining—not in some orderly, controlled fashion, but with a delight bordering on frenzy?

To "dance" anything—and for some of us, to dance *at all*—carries risk. It might be embarrassing. You might be humiliated. You might feel shamed by others. Giving yourself over to the risk, though, might also lead you to be among those who open themselves to what Rilke describes, at the poem's end, as the "happy" orange. Jesus didn't include this one in the proper "beatitudes" that made it into the Bible, but he might have added: *Blessed are those who dare to dance, for they shall live in delight.*

And yes: blessed are you when you risk delighting in your body, yielding to the deep appetite for pleasure you always carry within you. Blessed are you when you celebrate being alive in your body, come what may. Blessed are you who dare to open *yourself* by "peel[ing] fragrance upon fragrance" as you taste that "happy fruit." Blessed are you when you savor the beauty of this life and sense something of its sacrifice, finding yourself drenched with gratitude: for "it converted itself deliciously toward you." You *are* poet enough for this!

To dance the orange is to delight in and through your body, to discover it as a temple of the joying spirit. It is to risk "living everything," opening your life with an attentiveness that shapes your poet's mind. It is to embrace the wholeness of the present moment that does not depend upon your efforts or intentions. This is simplicity itself. This is eternal childhood made more precious still when we know that not just childhood but all of life is fleeting. To dance the orange—or anything else in your life? To love with your whole heart? To be fully alive in your body, with all that delights you? To know and inhabit the present moment with this kind of exuberance? To "establish kinship / with the pure, resisting rind, / with the juice that fills the happy fruit"? What could matter more?

This simple act of celebrating your life in and through your body, of savoring the ways you can learn to delight in this life, might become a way into the very self-discovery you need—and crave. This might itself be the gateway to what Jesus described as "the kingdom of heaven" which is always "among" us, opening to us in each moment, here and now. The dance might be fleeting, as Rilke concedes, and is often complicated by suffering and pain. Yet it is ever-present in your life as a possibility. A welcoming. An invitation. In the moment when you begin to open yourself to the call, you'll find yourself beginning to discover radiance—in *everything.* "Wait . . . , that's delicious"!

CHAPTER 11

OPENING TO REASSURANCE

I find you in all these things
that I cherish like a brother.
As seed you warm yourself in the least of things,
and give yourself to the greater things in their ripening.

This is the wondrous play of powers
moving through things to serve them:
in the roots growing, vanishing in the trunks,
and in the treetops like a rising from the dead.

—from *The Book of Hours*

[*STEPHANIE DOWRICK*]

Among the most challenging questions each of us must *live into* is whether we will survive circumstances that feel outside our control. Our happiness, future, even our fate might appear to rest on a single event or experience bending this way rather than that. It may also seem to depend on strengths or resilience that we doubt we have. As seriously, our wellbeing may seem to depend on the decisions other people are making *about* or *for* us—and, often enough, *against* us. Perhaps we are depleted, subject to painful self-criticism, or even blistering self-denigration. *"I can't endure this. It's too hard to find a way forward. Is there any meaning left in my existence? It is far, far too much."*

In the face of persistent fear, you will likely feel diminished and inadequate. Perhaps lost. It takes enormous energy to keep a mask of competence in place when that's not how you feel inside. How, then, do you, do we, restore balance within ourselves? How, then, do we regain hope, tap into our stores of resilience, or feel the truly magnificent regeneration the poem above promises?

Rainer Maria Rilke wrote this prayer-poem when he was just twenty-four years old. It has to be a work of instinct, then, rather than of lived experience. In it, he speaks of a "wondrous play of powers." It's a gorgeous phrase, deepened lovingly by *moving through things to serve them*. There's a promise of purposefulness here as well as surprise. How, though, would you access that "play" when the very idea of powers seems to mock you? How do you welcome a "rising" into a more confident or self-compassionate state of mind when you feel burdened by difficulties seemingly more powerful than you are?

This is a poem that responds to nature's rhythms, to nature's powers of regeneration, and to the very human hope for a "resurrection"—not least, for a regaining of connection and awe.

I wonder, though, what response it finds in you?

Writing in the persona of a monk (despite the poet's far more sensual life choices), Rilke may have been celebrating his emergence as an adult—and a poet—out of the hidden "trunk" of what he experienced as a stultifying and sometimes wretched childhood. This, the poem seems to say, is the poet's moment, his time: "like a rising from the dead." But is it your time?

Time itself changes in a crisis. We enter the realm of the interminable. It is hard then to give much credibility to an assurance that "This too will pass." Other anodyne phrases like *It's sure to turn out for the best*, or *Everything happens for a reason*, will feel banal or trivializing. Our longing for reassurance may be greatest at the very moment we are least equipped to summon it up. Or to trust it when it is offered or articulated by others.

Finding the divine "you"—a sacred center, an all-loving God, or a personified life force—as this poem celebrates, may seem at such times unreal or mocking. You may feel ruffled by such a claim, and not soothed. Yet even the faintest longing for reassurance is worth nourishing.

As his poem edges forward, Rilke moves to the "ripening" in "greater things," or specific qualities that are already made manifest. Following the arc of this poem, he—and we—leave the immaturity of childhood behind us, knowing that we will inevitably go beyond *ripening*—becoming more mature or powerful—toward decay, which is also part of, and intrinsic to, life.

> This is the wondrous play of powers
> moving through things to serve them:
> in the roots growing, vanishing in the trunks,
> and in the treetops like a rising from the dead.

Here, the poem takes us briefly to a place of darkness that's unexpectedly fecund: *in the roots growing, vanishing in the trunks.* Much of our growing *is* out of sight, unconsciousness only gradually made conscious. And sometimes emerging from confusion, lostness, bleakness, darkness. Poetry, with its inwardness, helps here. Reassurance may also help, even when it comes "wearing strange disguises," as I wrote in an earlier book.

Can you be gentler, then, and more patient in your self-understanding? However alone you feel in your suffering, it does not occur in a vacuum. Ours are societies unbalanced by extreme jittery, judging, insatiable extroversion, as well as a commitment to mid-adolescent dualistic thinking which can become so entrenched that many assume it to be inevitable.

It is common to conclude that if everything isn't totally right, then it has to be totally wrong. A more nuanced, contemplative way of being is easily scorned. And yet we persist. The invitation of this book is part of that persistence, which is also a resistance to what is superficial, mindlessly distracting, or numbing. Our writing, your reading: together we make a difference that didn't start with Rilke and won't finish with us, either.

A drive for reassurance is something basic to our human nature, although we experience and express that need differently. Sometimes what confronts us is fleeting and relatively trivial. "A tincture of time" or a dash of Stoicism may take care of it. Sometimes, though, it feels like—and might well be—a matter of the endurable or agonizingly unendurable. Or even a question of life or death.

More commonly, a drive for meaningful reassurance emerges when it feels as though our inner "architecture" has failed us. We are no longer on solid ground within ourselves. Our most persistent feelings are direly uncomfortable. We may feel trapped by insecurity, inadequacy, and confusion. Our inner monologue will do little to console us here: *What will happen if…? What will happen when…? How will I go on without…?*

We may ask of others, "What do you think?" "What would you do if you were me?", each time forgetting that our most profound source of wisdom lies within us—if only we could trust that. Or remember it.

Concerns about loved ones may be just as difficult to bear. Perhaps more so. Powerlessness looms large here. A child, spouse, friend, lover, or family member may be suffering beyond *their* bearing. Yet we can't reassure them that life will surely get better, knowing as we do that it might not. Words of reassurance may come to our lips, then fade there. Or perhaps we say them aloud, only to see our loved one protest their hurt, recoil, or turn away.

When reassurance fails, we lose connectedness. ("You can't help me. No one can help me.") Perhaps more painfully still, we may lose trust in our own inner world, in our capacity to endure, in that "play of powers," as Rilke names them. Reasons for self-abandonment are many. They often arise from anxiety, depression, isolation, inner turmoil, or despair. They may be a response to the existential crises we face, individually or collectively. Individually, they speak of a loss of self-love and an urgent need for active self-compassion. But how do you harvest such compassion when a basic reassurance that "All shall be well" is spoken in a language you have ceased to comprehend?

When reassurance for yourself feels fake or non-existent, you need positive connections with others more than ever. But to step into a communal space of any kind may seem a bridge far too far until you have regained some trust (and resilience) within your own self. It may help to discover that *your power to reassure others* is itself life-giving. Consciously choosing to be a reassuring, encouraging presence for others *is or can be* stabilizing. It is also fundamental to comprehending our elemental connectedness with those around us. We can influence their well-being; they can influence ours.

*

Reassurance is given or shown as much through gesture, atmosphere, and gaze as it is through words. It can come as a hug, a willingness to make time, a thoughtful reminder that you care and that *the other person's life matters.* That longing for reassurance together with a drive to offer it is something we share with other species. If you have ever had a family pet that you deeply loved you will know that reassurances seldom go one way. As we pat, soothe, murmur, calm, stroke a beloved or agitated creature, we are also reassuring ourselves. *I care. I am a caring person. Your need moves me. I want to meet it.*

That deep, primal longing to be reassured and to reassure is at least partially met by this poem. Could you try speaking it aloud, translating the "you" into what feels like a stable centering lifeforce image for you?

> I find you in all these things
> that I cherish like [kinfolk].
> As seed you warm yourself in the least of things,
> and give yourself to the greater things in their ripening.
> [*Pause, now. Simply pause. And then...*]
> This is the wondrous play of powers
> moving through things to serve them:
> in the roots growing, vanishing in the trunks,
> and in the treetops like a rising from the dead.
>
> As seed you warm yourself in the least of things,
> and give yourself to the greater things *in their ripening* [my
>   italics].

To observe the natural rhythms of *ripening*—the deeper levels of aliveness that exist around and within us—we must be capable not only of valuing life, but also of pausing.

The porousness of poetry and its sparseness assist this. Patterns of hectic busy-ness and displaced anxiety erode joy in many lives. Perhaps it helps to view reassurance, whether through words, insights, or gestures, as a gift of lovingkindness: from us to others; from others to us; from ourselves to ourselves. "Throw me to the wolves," said the Stoic philosopher, Seneca, "and I will come back leading the pack."

We may not all emerge from wolf-land quite so flamboyantly, but the ancient Roman philosopher's point is convincing. Some situations *can* be turned around. At every moment, the dynamics of our existence are changing. Why not for the better? It is also a reminder that whatever is here *now* is already passing. Holding on, grasping—whether to anxieties or fear of change—defies the momentum of existence. *All things are passing*, those "things" you treasure as well as those things you dread. We live in the flow of change, amid the inevitable forces of mortality. And, in that flow, you come to sense, perhaps, that yes: *you are the future.*

Reassurance is a signal to look to a bigger picture: to see *this moment* as part of a more spacious whole. It releases the trapdoor of obsessive thinking. It is a reminder that you add up to far more than your feelings, no matter how consuming those feelings may be.

Babies, small children, people of any age who are frightened, in shock or ill, the dying, the confused or bereft; all in any state of fragility; those who are unsure, insulted, bereft: all need reassurance. *We all* need reassurance. We all need soothing in times of fear, disappointment, or disruption. We each have our own pattern of anxieties. No one is exempt. Certainly, Rilke was not. We benefit when we possess at least some confidence that we are *available* to be reassured, as well as being capable of reassuring others. Rilke understood this need and acted on it—as in a consolatory letter he wrote to a grieving friend, reminding her that "[w]here things become truly difficult and unbearable, we find ourselves in a place already close to its transformation." That place is, with Rilke, never "beyond." It is here and now. Always.

*

The availability to be reassured is less universal than you might imagine. When people have suffered dreadfully, when their trust has been repeatedly betrayed or they have misplaced their faith in humanity or even themselves, they may well retreat inwardly and decisively. For them, a *reaching toward* may feel like a threat, not a reassurance. In *The Noonday Demon*, his remarkable personal study of depression, Andrew Solomon writes: "When you are depressed, the past and future are absorbed entirely by the present moment, as in the world of a three-year-old. You cannot remember a time when you felt better, at least not clearly; and you certainly cannot imagine a future time when you will feel better."

Depression is a cruel robber taking some of that from us. So do anguish, anxiety and self-doubt, as well as physical exhaustion, that come with persistent low moods. It is no surprise that depression is one of the most prevalent chronic illnesses of our time. It is also no surprise that there is not a single Western nation that's not trailing badly in meeting the needs of those suffering this complex, debilitating, and sometimes life-threatening illness.

Understanding that reassurance is sometimes impossible to receive invites us to be more generous about others' suffering, or our own. When we are in good shape, it may be enough for a loved one to give a hug and say, "Don't worry. We'll get through this." When we are not in good shape, such words may be received and heard as a lack of understanding that causes further pain or distancing.

So much depends not on mood alone but also on that moveable feast we call "a sense of self." A driving question for which there is no easy answer is, "Who are you when you are entirely alone?" My close friend and writing companion, Jane R. Goodall, reminded me that this was the question that took Rilke into a period of extreme isolation in the Castle Duino, a building full of enormous, empty spaces—and ghosts.

Jane wrote to me in a note, "I first discovered Rilke through his novel, *The Notebooks of Malte Laurids Brigge*, which I read during a very distressed period of young adulthood, and it was almost as if the *Notebooks* took me somewhere that released me from the prison of personal anxiety and the tyranny of a self largely formed in social and professional frameworks. I read and re-read it many times."

I am aware from my own periods of serious illness, and from observing grievous suffering in those I love—where life itself becomes fragile—that as great as your need seems to be, the suffering itself leaves cruelly little room for anything else. *The simplest of gestures are enough.* Words may be too much. The reassurers themselves need reassurance: "*Your constancy of presence, of devotion, of fidelity, are everything.*"

*

Rilke was a man loved and admired by many people. But his letters and more public writing show that, while he was largely generous in reassuring others, he himself could take in reassurances from very few. At the end of his life, when he desperately wished not to die at the age of fifty-one, it was the presence of his first great and perhaps only love, Lou Andreas-Salomé, that Rilke wanted, not his wife, Clara, nor his daughter, Ruth.

With all the sympathy in the world for Clara and Ruth (who longed to be with him), many of us will understand the reassurance that some people bring us without words, simply by their presence. Rilke had long before projected onto Lou almost magical powers of understanding and "knowing" what he needed.

Lou Andreas-Salomé was a psychoanalyst, indeed one of the earliest. She had prodigious personal charm and when Rilke fell in love with her, their significant age difference—she was born in 1861, Rilke in 1875—would have likely made her seem astonishingly worldly to him. A highly educated, brilliant woman, she was experienced by Rilke as profoundly, necessarily different from his clinging, insecure mother.

At the age of twenty-one, young René Maria—not yet Rainer, a change he made at Lou's urging—wrote in a letter to her that "Leaving you, through rain-dark streets / I steal quickly and feel / that everyone whose eyes meet mine / can see blazing in them / my blissful, resurrected soul." His dependence on Lou's understanding and reassurance may seem unusually heightened, revealing much about his vulnerability.

In late December of 1911, after finishing *The Notebooks of Malte Laurids Brigge*, his single novel, he wondered "Can you understand that in the wake of this book I have been left behind like a survivor, stranded high and dry in my innermost being, doing nothing, never to be occupied again?" But if his dependence was great—and difficult for Lou to bear—so was his gratitude for those qualities of reassurance he would continue to need long after they were in each other's daily lives.

*

Even without Rilke's depth of dependence on Lou, you don't have to be a public person or a poet to know instinctively that few people will "read" you wholly, and many truly well-meaning people will freely offer you ardent reassurances that utterly fail to hit the spot.

During my own recent years of complicated illness, several friends insisted on telling me how well I was looking. They also wanted to convince me how brave or "incredible" I was. (I was neither, nor did I look remotely well.) Did they want to reassure *themselves* that I would get through and not die? Perhaps. Certainly, their words were well-meant. But as beleaguered as I was, those same words made me feel unseen and unmet. One particularly good friend told me how well-rested I looked when I ached with exhaustion and couldn't take a step without pain. He intended nothing but kindness. Yet these were instances of good-hearted people seeing not "me" but the "brave, not-dying" person they needed me to be.

*

In a similar situation in your own life, faced with your need to reassure a loved one and unsure of what to say, it may be far safer to choose a more neutral path rather than insisting, *I know you will get through this.* Or attempting to make light of the other person's suffering—and, perhaps, the fear of illness and death it provokes in you.

Many people will hope to reassure a friend or loved one by telling them long stories of others who have been through what they regard as similar events. Or by becoming over-involved in the drama and their desire to "help." Or perhaps ranting and blaming a cruelly unfair world *Why should this happen to you, of all people...?* When the matter isn't too serious, venting does little harm and may even lead to laughter and relief. When the matter is serious, though, reaching into the very fabric of someone's existence, something more conscious and respectful is needed. A worthwhile question hovers: *Are you reassuring the other person, or yourself?*

Maturity demands we accept that there are very real differences between us when it comes to recovering or moving on from a real blow, whether that is to the body or the soul.

> I find you in *all these things*
> *that I cherish* [my italics], like a brother.
> As seed [or sacred potential] you warm yourself in the least of
>   things,
> and give yourself [your own self/selfhood/vitality] to the
>   greater things in their ripening.

It is profoundly freeing to be able to calm or talk ourselves down from catastrophizing, from running the worst possible scenarios repeatedly in our minds, and to hold onto some sense of proportion when we feel engulfed. But how?

Such strengthening must come from within: from the place where we receive the poet's words. And add our own responses. When a poem like this one speaks to us, it bypasses our defences and realigns us with belonging. We are part of all "these things" in which a primal *you* can be found. That *experiencing*—well beyond intellectual appreciation—can help us trust our powers, even in the face of a blow or what we regard as a shaming misstep. One way of understanding this is to see it as a ripening: a gradual emergence both in "the least of things" and in the "greater" ones—as a coming into wholeness. By expanding our sense of the possible, and *our own meaningful place in the larger scheme of things*, the depth of true poetry comes into its own. And we with it, discovering what abundance such poetry offers us.

Poetry of the kind we are experiencing—and not just *reading* here—helps us see the subtle and the great as coexistent. It challenges the frantic urgency of our fears, softening our need to make things right when they feel all wrong, or to pin down the predictable in the face of uncertainty.

*

True poetry will not and cannot always reassure. Paradoxically, that is itself reassuring. Some losses and many horrors lie outside reassurance's most generous reach. Nonetheless, poetry that speaks to truth's power challenges any separateness from one another and from a full acceptance of ourselves. American poet Muriel Rukeyser points to this when she concedes that "The fear of poetry is that we are cut off from our own reality."

Using far fewer words than prose or commentary, an authentic poem brings a pause, a nudge to listen, and perhaps to surrender and listen again, with increasing trust that we have inwardness to call on that will reveal itself when it is needed. And welcomed.

It's likely from those inner depths, rather than from others' reassurances, that hope can be kept alive. Or reborn. "Hope is not something we have," says Australian playwright and actor, Nakkiah Lui. "Hope is something we create." Nakkiah is my son Gabriel's wife, and the mother of my youngest grandchild. I am moved by her words. Yet I also know that some of us are innately more hopeful than others are, perhaps also more available to offer or receive reassurance. Some of us have had to bear less...and are less worn down. Some of us, conversely, have far more reason to be hopeful than our neighbors might. Nonetheless, the notion that hope is something we can create or encourage within ourselves fits

my experience of reading Rilke. That mysterious process of inner inspi-
ration when something "strikes us" is itself reassuring. Our minds—con-
scious and unconscious—are so much more richly resourced than we
generally allow for.

*

Whenever I return to this poem, as I often do, I am struck by the every-
where-ness of life within it: *I find you in* all *these things that I cherish*…
Wholeness is not named here; it is exemplified. Cherishing life—as a
brother or a sister might, with a sibling's familiarity—we observe boldly.
We come up close. Your breath meets mine. We resist indifference.

There is innocence and gentleness in those first words in German: *Ich
finde dich in allen diesen Dingen*…I find you in all these things…As you
sound aloud the four syllables of *Ich finde dich* you may likely also hear, as
if in echo, the four syllables of *Ich liebe dich* (I love you), both statements
of unassailable affection. Moreover, I am uplifted by the sense of agency in
this "I": *you* are there to be found; *I am here finding you.*

Holding a thread of my connection to the Whole has served me
best in my most frightening times: *I am not alone.* This reassurance can
change everything. This takes us to a central image in the poem: *as seed
you warm yourself in the least of things.* We are onto something marvelous
here, an affirmation not just of "being" but also "becoming." The phrase
becomes the locus of fecundity, of warmth, as the womb is. And in "the
least of things"? How effectively that challenges a reluctance to under-
stand or embrace humility, even as we may unfairly put ourselves down.
Within each seed, within every potent moment, life awaits us. Each seed,
however small, contains the future "whole"—the oak tree in the acorn,
the fruiting tree in the seed. The adult in the child. *You are the future.*

Sources in various religious and spiritual traditions explore the
potential meaning of a seed and the great reassurance this can bring.
From Buddhism we are assured that the source of all the great qualities
lives innately within us—including hope and renewal. We are invited

to trust that our original nature offers us everything that we need for an awakened life. That's a mighty thing: *we already have what we need.* Is that not the ultimate reassurance?

One of the wisest, most loving peace-teachers of our time, Vietnamese Zen teacher, poet, and monk Thich Nhat Hanh, wrote in *Living Buddha, Living Christ*: "We are all pregnant with the potential [the seed] for awakening." With that awareness, we become freer to water those seeds, those sacred potentials, and let them sprout, grow, bloom. Without awareness of that sacred seed—belonging in and to us all, *whoever we are*—we are more inclined to neglect the potential of that inner self. In ourselves and others.

You and I come to know that inner source through dreams, poetry, music, the rhythms of nature where we catch reflections of ourselves and what is beyond ourselves. We know it, too, through quietly observing our patterns of response to others—including the giving and receiving of reassurance. And by daring to know ourselves as well as others more compassionately and truthfully.

In the form of this poem as found in Mark's *Prayers of a Young Poet*—the only English translation of Rilke's original version—we find Rilke's note written as if a journal entry by the "monk" whom the poet imagined as the writing persona of poems that later became the opening part of *The Book of Hours*: "Just before falling asleep, this little poem came to him, and he recognized it with a smile."

A little poem "coming to him" is itself an experience of reassurance. Fresh inspiration "arriving" (from where?) always is at least this. But there's more. In American writer Robert Bly's rendition of the same poem, he took the liberty of adding words that were not Rilke's. His first line reads, "I find you in all these things *of the world*...". It is a liberty. Yet it is fair to assume that Bly was wanting to emphasize the presence of this creative force in *our* world, in *the world that is within us,* the one you and I are a part of.

Regeneration is ours to claim. We water it with our attention.

This is the wondrous play of powers

moving through things to serve them:
in the roots growing, vanishing in the trunks,
and in the treetops like a rising from the dead.

In the wondrous play of powers, *all* is not visible. Or "outer." The poet
takes us briefly, powerfully, to a place of darkness which is richly fecund:
in the roots growing, vanishing in the trunks. Much of our own growing is
out of sight, unconsciousness only gradually made conscious—not only
to others, but *to ourselves.* Ours is a time unbalanced by jittery, judging,
insatiable extroversion as well as a commitment to dualistic thinking
that can also split us off from ourselves.

Yet the poem itself brings a promise: strength grows upwards, begin-
ning with the seed and growing through roots. It is dependent upon the
richness of the soil and the faithfulness of attending. It vanishes in the
trunks—and at times within us—only to reappear like a resurrection, a
rising from the dead. In these brief lines, we are taken from seed to resur-
rection. From hiddenness to exuberance.

Only a rare poet could conjure this and make it true: *in the treetops,*
air meets the infinity that is sky. Earth, and what grows from the earth,
spreads itself in celebration. Eternity is *here* and *now.* In that bigger
vision of self, of life, you have nothing to prove. Nothing to grasp for.
You can afford to pause. To breathe. To trust. To be. This is not simply a
song *we* sing. It is one that sings *us.*

CHAPTER 12

FACING THE DARK

You, darkness that I come from,
I love you more than the flame
that bounds the world,
shining
as it does in some certain ring
beyond which no being knows of it.

But the darkness holds everything within itself:
forms and flames, animals and myself,
how it grasps them,
people and forces—
And it is possible that a great power
stirs in my neighborhood.
I believe in nights.

—from *The Book of Hours*

[*MARK S. BURROWS*]

The Hebrew scriptures announce the origins of creation with a poignant image: "In the beginning...darkness covered the face of the deep" (Genesis 1:1–2). God, as imagined in that ancient story, creates in the darkness, brings forth life out of a dark and "formless void." Yet to imagine darkness as a place of primal creativity, as the setting for the origins of all that is, is for many unsettling. For we often find ourselves disoriented in the dark, uneasy when we cannot see and have lost our visual bearings.

The fear it evokes is rooted deep within us, triggering that primal part of the human brain where the "fight or flight" instinct lives. It hardly seems something we might, with Rilke, address as an intimate friend:

> You, darkness that I come from,
> I love you more than the flame
> that bounds the world.

We guard ourselves against it, which is surely the main reason modern societies have bathed our public spaces with light. We love the flame and prefer the light to the darkness. And so we harness the light to protect ourselves, fearing the darkness for the ways it exposes our vulnerability. It can be deeply unnerving, leaving us feeling exposed, triggering our fear, heightening our sense of uncertainty. When we understand something, we often say, "*I see...*" and when we are confused, we speak of being "in the dark" about something we can't grasp.

In fact, most of us live in towns and cities awash with light, artificially brightened from dusk until dawn. Children who grow up in such conditions accept this state as normal. Many of them have never seen the Milky Way and cannot imagine the magnificent canopy of stars that stretches across the heavens like a dazzling blanket studded with sparkling diamonds. An article entitled "Our Vanishing Night" ran in *National Geographic* some years ago, reminding us of what we know: that an ever-increasing majority of humankind lives under "intersecting domes of reflected, refracted rays from over-lit cities and suburbs, from light-flooded highways and factories" to the point that "in most cities the sky looks as though it has been emptied of stars." In the face of this absence, as the author Verlyn Klinkenborg goes on to say, "we've lit up the night as if it were an unoccupied country."

All of this is understandable given how unsettling, and in some cases dangerous, the darkness can be. We lose our orientation in it. As children, many of us might have had a small night-light glowing in our bedrooms through the night as a source of comfort and security. In our later years, we find ourselves reluctant to walk down a dark alleyway at night, fearing the danger that might be awaiting us.

We'd rather stay in that well-lit room rather than venture forth into the unknown where we might lose our way. Or face threats, real or imagined, that might await us there—a difficult situation in our workplace; a wounding or even dangerous relationship; the disorientation of feeling lost in a large crowd. Darkness has many forms, some of them distinctly uncomfortable if not outright threatening. In such situations, few of us would find ourselves singing, with the familiar opening of the hit-song from the mid-1960s, "hello darkness, my old friend."

*

In one of her poems in which she wrote of the darkness—and there are many—Emily Dickinson remarks that "[w]e grow accustomed to the Dark – / When Light is put away," which makes sense to us. Except when it doesn't. But she goes on to point to those

> larger – Darknesses –
> Those Evenings of the Brain –
> When not a Moon disclose a sign –
> Or Star – come out – within –.

Darkness also has an inner face. Indeed, we have within ourselves "a formless void" where darkness "hovers over the deep." What are we to do with such "evenings of the brain" when we feel lost and alone, depressed, or desperate? When we feel a panic or dread that has no easy remedy? When the walls seem to be closing in on us? Such "larger darknesses" comes in many forms, gripping us in times of loss and loneliness. Leaving us feeling disoriented. Bringing on waves of panic that enervate us altogether to the point that we feel utterly incapacitated.

In the face of all this, what could Rilke possibly mean in a poem that reads like a love song to darkness? What might have prompted him to address the darkness with the intimate German form of "you"—"You, darkness that I come from..."? Did that leave you confused when you first read it? Or relieved? Did you feel a sense of confusion or affirmation—or perhaps some mix of both? When I first read this poem in my late teens, now many years ago, I could make little sense of it, and yet I somehow knew that it held meaning that was important. That it pointed to something I would eventually come to discover.

When I now return to the poem, I can see that it voices the inner longings—the mirror-side of loss—that gripped Rilke as an impressionable and sensitive young man. A few years after writing this poem, he expressed this boldly in one of his celebrated *Letters to a Young Poet*:

> We have no reason to mistrust the world, for it is not opposed to us. If it has fears, they are *our* fears; if it has abysses, these belong to us; if there are dangers, we must learn to love them. And if we were to arrange our lives according to the principle that advises us to face what is difficult, we'll find that what is most alien to us will become the most trusted and true things in our lives.

Does such a passage suggest Rilke's foolish naivete, or does it express a counterintuitive wisdom? Or, perhaps, a little of both? If the latter, how do we integrate the creative power of such a claim into our lives? Here there are no easy answers. And it took Rilke, as it has taken me, years to cultivate the work of embracing his wise advice that "we must learn to love [the dangers]" we face. That journey begins when we find the courage to face the darkness in our lives bravely, no longer as a menace to be avoided but as something that has the power to destroy *and* to create, to tear down *and* to allow life to come forth.

In his memoir of depression, *Darkness Visible*, William Styron chronicles his dangerous drift into what he calls "the gray drizzle of horror." After managing to hold his long affliction with depression at bay,

tempered by alcohol and incessant work, it finally rose up with destruc-
tive power in his life, becoming so severe that he wrote of it as "madness."

When his book appeared in 1990, I was on the verge of my own
plummet into some of those "larger darknesses" Dickinson named, a
decline made all the more incredible—first of all to myself and only later
to others—by the fact that my life at that point had seemed an outward
success. This all made the depression that was beginning to overcome
me utterly unintelligible and debilitating. I should add that I could not
read Styron's book when it came into my hands, consigning it to a corner
of my bookshelf where it remained for years until I began to find the
courage to face my own version of what he called his "storm of murk."

At the time, I could not have affirmed with Rilke that this most diffi-
cult of experiences was something I should embrace as "the most trusted
and true thing" in my life. In the lowest point of that downward spiral,
when the very fabric of my public and private life seemed on the verge of
unravelling, as it subsequently did, I could not have imagined Rilke's love
of darkness. I survived it in a kind of stupor of numbness, assuaged by a
series of reckless decisions. Nor could I have echoed his bold confession
that "I believe in nights." Everything I had been raised to believe and trust
had to do with denying such a conviction. In this, of course, I was—and
am—hardly alone, reared as I was in a society allergic to the "unmanaged"
life. This tendency prompted C. G. Jung's comment that America was "like
a house without a basement," leaving no room for the dark moorings of the
unconscious where creativity dwells.

*

Strong poems like this one open windows into dimensions of human
experience that we might not otherwise have come to know. They
startle us against the grain of our flimsy certainties. They might even
remain baffling to us as the years pass. And yet they do not let us go,
and we can only hope to live into the wisdom they carry and reveal in
time. And let me say this again, as I have elsewhere: poems like this
take time. They call us to listen into the silences of that "formless void"

we carry within us. They require space until we can begin to peer into their depths and glimpse the insights they bear—and discover what might await us there.

This has been my experience with this poem. I knew amid my own fears and failures, uncertainties and disappointments, that this was a poem that I would have to live my way into. That expectation was not wrong. The poem has been one of those that would not let me go through the tumble of years that followed. It refused to be silenced by my fickle hope to "manage" my life by choosing to remain in the light, as it were—by choosing to love not the darkness but "the flame / that bounds [my] world."

The poem's opening addresses darkness with a tender intimacy and cautious acknowledgement, even respect. What the poet seems to know was the truth that the darkness of disorientation and loss was not the end of life, and also not the antithesis to creativity. It was—and is—one of the unavoidable conditions we find ourselves, often unavoidably, facing.

My experience of those "larger darknesses" might well be different from yours. But I presume that there is something we all share in this journey, a common experience we find ourselves having, even if the circumstances that bring this on are unique. What we do know of them, though, is that they can overwhelm us to the point that we feel suffocated. They traumatize us, cripple our sense of agency, and leave us despondent. The Spanish mystic, John of the Cross, described the sense of abandonment this can evoke within us as "the dark night of the soul."

Rilke knew the destructive power of darkness in his own life. Yet here, in this poem, he also sees another, potentially creative dimension that it can bring our way. Darkness can point to what might initially seem to be a kind of sightless chaos, at least on the surface, but in its depths something else is at least potentially at work in those "larger darknesses" we face within, which can initially feel utterly overwhelming. Like a force over which we have little or no control, which threatens to undo us—and might—leaving us feeling as if we had stumbled into a dead end without hope of return.

Rilke sensed that the darkness, whatever else we might experience it to be, "holds everything within itself." Everything. He goes on to name several—"forms and flames, animals and myself"—by which he means all that is in this creaturely world we inhabit. Including the light. He goes on to wonder about "how it grasps them, / people and forces—" and we begin to sense that he sees the dark as holding the potential for life. And that the creative life often arises in the dark, in the midst of that "faceless void" in which "darkness cover[s] the face of the deep."

As the drama of creation unfolds, following this ancient mythic account, everything that came to be emerged from out of this darkness: the light, waters and land, vegetative and animal life in all its myriad diversity, and finally humanity. Everything came "from darkness," which "held" everything. Everything.

As Rilke goes on to conclude in the closing lines,

> And it is possible that a great power
> stirs in my neighborhood.

I loved these lines when I first read them, and over time they became etched in my memory: *Und es kann sein: eine große Kraft / rührt sich in meiner Nachbarschaft.* The blend of boldness and humility is remarkable: "And it is possible...." As is the tenderness of his description, bringing all this cosmic force into the intimacy of "home" and the familiarity of place, "...that a great power / stirs in my neighborhood."

"It is possible": these words open a crease of openness where we can imagine, at least, something we have not experienced. After all, when we find ourselves lost in dread or spiraling downward into the depths of depression, assertions of any sort—no matter how sensible—bring no comfort and offer little help. No, *it is possible* that "a great power" is stirring close to me, in my own neighborhood. And yours. Which might well be a condition of overpowering fear or incapacitating shame—a "place" somewhere deep within you. "It is possible that a great power / stirs" *here* and *now*. In those "larger darknesses" of your experience.

*

"It is possible": as you face that inner darkness, you can also begin to meet it as a place of discovery. As one that invites you to move beyond the stifling pressures of fear and dread, to settle into a more spacious receptivity. Rilke spoke of this in his later poems as "the Open," by which he meant a certain kind of availability to the world around us, and to our place within it; a heightened awareness that we belong to "the Whole," together with everything else in this world—and first of all, in our own "neighborhood."

The wisdom of this insight expanded what Rilke pointed to in his novel, *The Notebooks of Malte Laurids Brigge*, commenting that he found himself in the middle of his life, as if for the first time, "learning to see":

> I don't know where this comes from, but I find that everything is now touching me more deeply than before, no longer staying at the place where it once came to an end. I have an inner life that I previously did not know about. Everything now goes to that depth. And I don't really understand what happens there.

Think about it: the "inner life" is sheltered from the light with its outward energies. Its depths are not accessible by means of the managing mind. Rilke's description of this is filled with disavowals: "I don't know..." and "I don't really understand what happens there." Because it is not about knowing, at least not in the way we "know" things with our eyes and try to control them with our thoughts. The nights we experience, those "inner darknesses" we face, can leave us languishing with the uncertainties of not-knowing.

And yes, "it is possible" that the feeling of being unsettled can also slow you down and invite your curiosity. Call out to you to greet life with trust. To welcome it with a sense of wonder. To give yourself over from complaint to curiosity—as Rilke does here, admitting that learning to see can awaken us to what we do not, and perhaps cannot, know. To open yourself to sense that the integrity of your life lies in the depths, beyond the surfaces, deeper than what your outer vision can reach. That something more, something other is necessary for you to discover the inner depths of your heart.

We often only gradually find that this is something that happens within us, apart from our intentions. That it is not something we manage with our will. "It is possible that a great power / stirs in [your] neighborhood." But to grasp it, to be grasped by it, you must resist the seduction of fickle certainties and renounce the lure of wishful thinking. To do this calls for courage, the courage to listen and wait in what one medieval writer called "the cloud of unknowing."

*

In "Wuxing," an ancient Chinese philosophical approach known as the "five elements theory," water is named as one of the constitutive elements, along with fire, earth, metal, and wood. This tradition identifies water with the darkness and cold of winter. But the quiet of winter, this time of dormancy, is necessary for the quickening of our creative life. We need the "rest" that seeds need as they lie in dark soil. We need the quiet to send our own roots down into the depths of our soul, seeking as they do the moist, generative soil that is impenetrable by light.

The generative forces of nature depend on this darkness. And, yes, the seed will also send up shoots that will rise from the earth's depths toward the light. This rising has an inevitably that is as sure as the gravity that pulls all things downward. But it is just as important to realize that the power of this rising has everything to do with the downward-reaching roots as they seek the depths, hidden far from the light.

"And it is possible that a great power / stirs" close by, "in my neighborhood" as he puts it. In these depths, the "inner life" can have its way with us and in us—often enough against our thin desires and plans. Rilke is surely right in admitting that even when he sensed something of this, he could not "understand" what was going on there. Except that he *knew* that this creative surge was having its way with him, in his inner life.

Rilke recognized this creative power as bringing about a kind of "ripening," another favorite word in his poetic lexicon. This points to the soul's life-force that is within us, but by no means dependent upon us with all our competencies and strengths. Only in our weakness, only when we have acknowledged our "unknowing," with all its vulnerabilities, only when we set aside the defining powers of our minds, do we discover within ourselves the "formless void" of the heart where we begin to "undefine" ourselves. To open ourselves to the disorientation that creates room for what we do not yet know, for what we are still becoming. To discover, beyond the cliche that we *have* a future, that we *are the future*.

*

"You, darkness that I come from": what a startling opening this is. Perhaps it is one we only begin to understand as we learn to face the "larger darknesses" we carry within ourselves—as bottomless as these feelings sometimes seem—with a certain curiosity. Even here, Rilke is sure that the darkness is not simply a problem to be solved. It is also—or it can become for us—a mystery to be discovered.

If that is so for you, whatever resistance you might also feel, try risking making a beginning here. Dare to imagine that power "stirring" close to you. In your "neighborhood," yes, but even more so *within* you. Within *you*. Even when those "larger darknesses" feel ready to overwhelm you, as they often do. The courage required to take this first step is never easy. First steps rarely are. But as you turn yourself toward that darkness, as you turn to face it with whatever slender trust you can find, you might begin to discover what Rilke did late in his life when he declared, in the Seventh Elegy:

> Nowhere, beloved, will it be world as it is within. Our
> life goes forth in transformations.

In such a moment you might begin to discover, as Rilke put it in one of the *Sonnets to Orpheus*, how

that shaping spirit which masters the earthly
loves in the figure's swing nothing as much as the turning
point. (II.12)

And yes, if Rilke is right, if the darkness "holds everything" within itself, then it always holds the power of change—for you, even in those times or seasons of your life when you seem lost in the dark.

For the darkness that we often experience as a despairing place can also be one of liminality. We can discover it as a "borderland," one that carries a generative and creative power. It took me many years to say, as Rilke did in *The Book of Hours*, that

I love the dark hours of my life,
which deepen my senses.

But over time I did begin to trust what he meant later in the same poem when he affirmed that from such "hours" came

...the knowing that I have
room for a second life, timeless and wide.

When we find ourselves in such "dark hours" or seasons of our lives, when our senses are on high alert, we can begin to become more aware of how we "belong" to "the Whole," with all our vulnerabilities. We can begin to attune ourselves differently, through a necessary "unknowing," to the life we carry within us and the world of which we are an inviolable part.

Such moments can become turning points, by which I mean inter-ruptions to your settled ideas of yourself and the world that might orient you differently—toward yourself and others. True, they might not have changed anything in and of themselves. But by reminding you that your life "goes forth in transformations," they invite you to trust that you can walk in a new direction. With a new sense of your own agency, knowing that you belong to "the Whole" with the one precious life that is yours. *For you are the future.*

Such turnings beckon you to sense your part in a spaciousness that is present, here and now, in the creativity you always carry within yourself. For life "brims with transformations," as Rilke put it in one of the late *Sonnets to Orpheus*. Even when that seems unlikely or even impossible. What, then, of the darkness? He goes on to end this poem with a startling confession that comes as close to a personal creed as the poet ever came. But he comes to this only after affirming darkness as the intimate "other" in our lives, the divine "you" who is our origin, and after claiming that this darkness holds *everything* within its grasp, including *you*. For the darkness, your darkness, is not only a place to fear. It is the face of ongoing creation in the hidden depths of this life, of your life. And, with bold strokes the poet sees this as what holds "everything" together. *Everything.* Including your life, with all its vulnerabilities and fears, amid all you worry and wonder about.

Why darkness? Perhaps because the darkness demands that we slow down. That we look carefully. That we wait patiently and trust cautiously. It calls for our patience, and perseverance, beyond the pressures of the workday. It invites us to open ourselves to the rhythms that inevitably seem to bring forth light from the darkness of the night. It is the cradle of solitude, that state when all that we have managed during the day unravels in unforeseen ways and we open ourselves to change.

This is what animates Rilke's identifying darkness with the source of creativity, not simply as a burden you might need to endure. He raises the stakes by singing out the melody of his deepest longing: "You, darkness...I love you more than the flame / that bounds the world...."

This is a remarkable claim, to be sure. And Rilke wants to be certain to say that this is not *only* about you. It is about you along with all that is, for

> ... the darkness holds *everything* within itself:
> forms and flames, animals and myself,

> how it grasps them,
> people and forces...

Darkness is the seedbed of the soul. And as Rilke suggests, it holds *everything* within itself. Including you, even in your most difficult hours. What else is there to do, then, but to open yourself to this wellspring, to give yourself to the darkness where you find yourself invited to be made anew—again and again? As you begin to sense this truth within yourself, you might try repeating Rilke's simple creed as you repeat his words quietly to yourself with as deep a conviction as you can muster: "*I believe in nights.*"

CHAPTER 13

CURIOSITY AND CONFUSION

I live my life in widening rings
that spread out to encompass all things.
I may not bring the last to completion,
but I will surely try.

I'm circling around God, around the ancient tower,
and I've been circling for thousands of years,
and I don't yet know: am I a falcon, a storm,
or a vast song?

—from *The Book of Hours*

[*STEPHANIE DOWRICK*]

*I live my life in widening rings / that spread out to encompass all things…
And I don't yet know…* As I read those lines, favorites of mine in Rilke's
work, I am struck by the ever-increasing spaciousness the poet evokes,
as well as the thrilling potential of *not yet knowing.* Unsettling, uncertain,
and expansive all at once.

Rilke wrote those lines as a very young man. As a much older
woman I can confidently say that as we humans age, we will not remain
the same, no matter how blithely we may pretend this to be possible.
On this complex journey of aging, either we will contract—emotionally
and in our world view—or we will expand. We will become either more

habit-bound and resistant to change—or more open-minded and wel-
coming of new ideas and "widening rings."

This may not be entirely a matter of choice for you. It could very
much depend on the culture and context in which you were raised, then
go on to raise yourself and others. It may also depend on what values you
consciously prioritize. Self-placating statements such as *People like me* or
This is how we've always done it/voted/thought can be a reassurance. They
can also be inhibiting—for us and for those around us.

So, a question arises that is worth exploring—and living into. Can
we help ourselves if our orbits of experience and vision seem to be any-
thing but "widening"? Writing this book with Mark is testimony to my
belief that we can indeed "help ourselves" and do so successfully.

The same mind that can conjure up worst-case scenarios can equally
deliver intellectual, emotional, and spiritual "wealth." If we were together
in a real-time workshop, I might invite you, for example, to summon
up the well-wishing fairy godmothers of your infancy. Then, imagina-
tively, to place a supplementary order of the qualities and strengths *you
most need now.* This invitation could, as if through a magic-wand wave,
make your life calmer, more satisfying or more coherent. Or perhaps a
newly imagined life would be more vibrant, risky, bold, daring? Look
with interest at what your quick mind brings forward.

My own order to the fairy godmothers would be quite straightfor-
ward. The qualities I want to have—*right now*, please, and in greedy
abundance—are patience, musicality, and curiosity. Musicality is part of
what I love about poetry and the best prose writing. I'm talking cadence
here, rhythm and tenor, not rhyme. Patience is examined on many of
these pages and was central in the years-long creation of this book. That
last quality, though, curiosity, is what most preoccupies me.

Curiosity runs beyond a simplistic "why." It leaps outside the con-
fines of an instruction manual. Given rein, it bypasses the obvious and
the superficial. First-hand experiences of curiosity show *there is always
more to know* and every day offers a new experience—if we allow it to
do so. Curiosity lessens our fears of difference. In fact, it welcomes the

infinite variety in human cultures and capabilities. It can make "difference" exciting rather than confronting as we learn how much *we* share with others—and what we don't. Plus, what we can only discover in and through opening our minds to other realities.

I love it, too, that curiosity isn't satisfied by rote answers, by dogma, by what's formulaic or linear, expected or conventional. No true art is created without curiosity. It must have a stroke of originality, a sense of the "untried" and of the intimacy between "me" and "things that interest me."

The English writer E. M. Forster, born only a few years later than Rilke and himself very much an unconventional thinker, claimed curiosity's value unconditionally: "The four characteristics of humanism are curiosity, a free mind, belief in good taste, and belief in the human race," he wrote. "Good taste," with its judgmental bourgeois overtones, sits a little oddly here. Forster was, perhaps incredibly for contemporary readers, bold in his portrayal of characters who were "not English," and was strikingly cosmopolitan for the time. "The time," however, still (vilely) punished—and imprisoned—men for homosexuality.

*

The desire to know more, to investigate well beyond the obvious is a quality natural to most children across all cultures. Yet it's so easy to lose touch with this faculty as each child grows older. You may feel "it's all too much" and that you "can't be bothered" to step beyond the widely acceptable. Or that life is unbearably complex, and you want nothing but to retreat into the known.

Let us also not forget the powerful contemporary social imperatives to subdue our curiosity, and us with it. The primal myth of Adam and Eve in the Book of Genesis, driven from Eden because Eve tempted Adam with an apple from the Tree of Knowledge, follows Greek myths and other more ancient stories warning us against seeking knowledge to which we are somehow "unentitled." So does the story of Lot's wife, turned to salt after her backward glances at Sodom.

Yet despite ancient and contemporary pressures to keep our heads down and conform, many will persist in their seeking of meaning. "I *circle* God"… I do not "land." Certainly, I do not give up. In my own life and work, I recognize that it has been the hardest of circumstances that pushed me to experience how transformative as well as necessary deep enquiry can be. I'm not talking about categorical "answers" either. Or inviting you to seek a "final word." "No feeling is final," wrote Rilke elsewhere. No word is final either.

*

Curiosity exposes an expanding universe. It opens us to a vision of the universe that brings a renewed sense of our connectedness with it. It's a wake-up moment each time you experience curiosity's rush. It urges you to look further, without and within, to *live into what you question*— or what seems to be questioning *you*. The active interest that curiosity allows pushes you to observe the minute and subtle in our natural world. And, just as wonderfully, it pushes you in your emotional world to explore cause and effect—and their many deviations, including how it is that *you affect others* and not just how *they affect you*.

Much anguish in human relationships could be avoided if people were genuinely curious about their *own* motivations even more than about what motivates *others*—which we might endlessly unpick. Even more, we are helped by genuine curiosity about the *effect of our actions*.

"Look deeply" is a worthwhile mantra. *Pause*. Listen carefully, not just to your sometimes self-justifying thoughts but also to what others say—or do not say—in response.

As powerful as words are, actions are even more significant. Reading and writing *are* actions. This is where we can choose to be more conscious, and far more accountable.

> I live my life in widening rings …
> …I may not bring the last one to completion,
> *but I will surely try* [my italics].

*

Curiosity inquires through the senses, memory, free association, and emotions, at least as powerfully as it does through the intellect. Instinct is central here: *"I just knew there was something wrong...and had to find out. Or, I felt this choice was right.... even though it was never what I had in mind."* Curiosity makes us bolder than we might otherwise be. It refuses to be satisfied with tired habits or worn banalities. Or with the over-familiar demands or expectations of the status quo.

Be assured that I am not talking about prying into others' lives, asking prurient questions, or pushing others outside their comfort zone. We need our physical and emotional boundaries, children as much as adults. It's *our own* comfort zone, *our own* lack of awareness, that we can test fruitfully—and must do if we desire to grow, develop, and deepen our lives.

Jane Hirshfield, American poet and commentator on poetry, observes in *Ten Windows* that "too much certainty and single-mindedness irritates as well as bores; the idea that one can know what is right, or that a general truth is possible, is an insult to the real." Living beyond the limits of "generalities" is essential for our growth. It is also vital to cultivate generous families, communities, and nations. The future viability of our world depends on this.

Few of us will go as far as the genuinely original American writer, Annie Dillard, did in *Pilgrim at Tinker Creek* where she wrote:

> I have often noticed that these things, which obsess me, neither bother nor impress other people even slightly. I am horribly apt to approach some innocent at a gathering, and like the ancient mariner, fix him with a wild, glitt'ring eye and say, "Do you know that in the head of the caterpillar of the ordinary goat moth there are two hundred twenty-eight separate muscles?" The poor wretch flees. I am not making chatter; I mean to change his life.

There's an anarchic quality to a genuinely curious mind. It refuses to "stay in its lane." It defies authoritarianism, cheap sloganeering, or the premature conviction that any one ideologically driven group or individual could possibly have all the answers.

Curiosity allows for subtlety, complexity, and spaciousness—Rilke's "widening rings"—and the freedoms of mind that E. M. Forster so valued. It obviates the need to insist that someone else is wrong for you to feel in the right. It welcomes *more* and makes space for the *other*. How refreshing that is. And how vital if we are to live with one another with respect and care, honoring our interdependence rather than living in fear and hostility toward others.

Fundamentalist reactions or plain old obdurate thinking are brutal in the ways they shut people off from true dialogue. To forbid questions, to denigrate viewpoints that differ from your own: these are acts of violence. They betray relatedness. Ultimately, they silence the soul.

*

With curiosity, of course, comes risk—including the everyday risk of being wrong, of falling flat on your face, of making a "fool of yourself." Dare I say, "So what!"? Far better to fall than to live in such fear of your own failings that you retreat into muteness, melancholy, or self-hatred. Far better to repeat, "So what!" than to be a dogmatist whose ego-strength depends on being always right—and seeing those who think or live differently as always wrong.

No one is constantly "right." Not one of us is omniscient. Rilke's God is ever ripening—always "still becoming." Curiosity insists that no matter how expert someone may be, there is always more to discover. More to "live into"—with fullness of heart.

Franciscan priest and writer Richard Rohr points with humor and affection to what's needed to defeat our anxious grandiosity—to tame the ego and free the "shadow self." An image of oneself as always in the "right," or as "one of the chosen few," is a narcissistic response that blocks genuine self-acceptance and an embrace of wholeness, and robs us of our innate complexity, always unfolding.

Rohr writes in *Things Hidden: Scripture as Spirituality*:

> The ego wants to eliminate all humiliating or negative information in order to "look good" at all costs. Jesus calls this self an "actor," a word he uses fifteen times in Matthew's Gospel, though it is usually translated from the Greek as "hypocrite." The ego wants to keep us tied to easy and acceptable levels of knowledge. It does not want us going down into the "personal unconscious" or, in Jung's term, our "shadow self." The shadow includes all those things about ourselves that we don't want to see, are not yet ready to see, and don't want others to see. We try to hide or deny this shadow, most especially from ourselves.

*

Building up an inner story, a stable confidence in our interior world, is something we are guided toward by our environment. Where that environment is rich with interest and appreciation, we are profoundly fortunate. We can't explore outwards with zest until we have a sense of "self" to return to. I'm not a particular fan of e. e. cummings' poems, but I love the wisdom he shares in his reminder that "Once we believe in ourselves, we can risk curiosity, wonder, spontaneous delight or any experience that expresses the human spirit."

As I reflect on this, I am remembering the gifts of a childhood where wide-ranging reading was highly encouraged and the local public library was part of our lives. It clearly suited my parents (both teachers) that "the girls"—my older sister and I—were more than able to entertain ourselves as long as we each had a pile of books. We both still, decades later, "talk books" routinely and have piles of them around our homes, preferably many gems, not just one, still waiting to be read and frequently exchanged between us.

I also remember that, as precocious readers, we were allowed to borrow adult books from the library long before adolescence. But it was on the packed bookshelves in my family's modest first-floor apartment, in a simple block of four "flats" as we called them, that at the age of about seven or eight I found and read some pages at least from Bronislaw Malinowski's *The Sexual Life of Savages*. Given that I lived in one colonized country, Aotearoa/New Zealand, and we had recently returned from another, Western Samoa, this was probably a disastrous journey into knowing more about sex or, far worse, "savages." However, the silent triumph of at last finding something I probably "shouldn't" read is what has stayed with me. Not the content. It was a subversive act of curiosity that was my secret triumph.

*

Did I discover then that, way beyond the sexual realm, curiosity is a bodily experience as much as it is a cerebral one? *What am I observing here? What is stirring within me? What's that sensation? What does it evoke…? Where does this music take me? As I dance with new ease, what is my body recalling? As I recoil, what am I recoiling from? Why are some people so relaxed in these situations, and others so uptight? Where is my body supporting me? And where not? Will I ever have the confidence I believe I need?*

Emotions buried deep need respecting. They call for compassionate self-discovery. Curiosity can make life more wondrous, more interesting, without harshness or intrusiveness. It is our privilege to choose to become increasingly more skillful, empathic, and above all plain kinder to ourselves and others. Empathy requires that we check carefully: *If I am unusually curious about another person, is that for their sake? Or my own?*

The shadow of prurience dulls curiosity's freshness. At the opposite end of the shadow-spectrum loom apathy, ennui, cynicism, and indifference, all enemies of curiosity. How tragic it is, then, to see a child or young person already excluded from their own potential through learned habits of switching off their natural wondering. Or by choosing hectic, superficial entertainment only, thereby dulling themselves into helpless acquiescence.

Curiosity is essential to creativity, and creativity is vital to our survival as a species. But curiosity needs refining as well as encouragement. It needs affirming. *Knowledge itself needs valuing*, not as a commodity to increase our transitory "value" in the marketplace, but as a way of living and being.

*

It is a surprisingly useful question sometimes to ask yourself, "What am I *not* seeing?" It may also be worthwhile when you are between the proverbial "rock and hard place" to explore points of view or perspectives that differ from those to which you are most accustomed. What's most familiar may seem natural or inevitable yet may not be. *I'm circling around…God. I am encircling God. I am encircled, God. God, encircle me…* How musical language is when we surrender to it.

> I'm circling around God, around the ancient tower,
> and I've been circling for thousands of years,
> and I don't yet know: am I a falcon, a storm,
> or a vast song?

An empathic imagination can take you far, and for that not-knowing plays a vital part. Listening without preconceptions or limiting judgments, taking in what you (or others) see, hear, feel and reflecting upon it: this is what opens you to gain insight into the matchless diversity of our vast human family. And this is what might also bring patience.

When not much older than Franz Kappus, the "young poet" who became his correspondent, Rilke was not—I believe—backing away from curiosity and self-inquiry when he wrote these much-quoted words:

> Be patient toward all that is unresolved in your heart
> and try to love the questions themselves, like locked
> rooms and like books written in an utterly unknown
> language. Don't search now for the answers; they can't
> be given to you because you couldn't yet live them. And
> what matters is to live everything. Live the questions
> now. Perhaps on some future day you'll find yourself,
> slowly and imperceptibly, living into the answer....

There's excitement for me each time I read this passage, which voices an explicit call to much-needed patience. There is also a steadiness of trust in what *life itself* is teaching us, if we open ourselves with curiosity toward it and if we can allow for that. How easy it is to discount *what you have already gained in experience and knowledge.* That's the source of your unique path into a wiser and more spacious life: your own experiences, your own maturing reflections upon them. Not least through those events you would have done anything to avoid.

For "living everything," as Rilke urges, necessitates a trust in your very existence that can arise only from a depth of self-respect, one that accompanies a willingness to live honestly. And with courage.

> I live my life in widening rings
> that spread out to encompass all things.
> I may not bring the last to completion,
> but I will surely try.

Grounding your insights in lived experience is how you make ideals real. Most of us will gain wonderfully through learning to "read" nature, noting and responding to seasonal changes, landscapes, to town or city forms. Noting, also, with the wonderment of a child, how the world of which we are a part acts on us and within us. This is a way to see your own *human nature* within the vastly dynamic complex we call the natural world. It is also a way to see your life as part of the seen and unseen Whole. As African American writer and Nobel Prize winner, Toni

Morrison, concluded, "At some point in life, the world's beauty becomes enough." That sentence is a poem.

*

Poetry worth reading invariably supports a greater spaciousness of seeing. Seeing into. Seeing through. Seeing beyond. Jane Hirshfield, in *Ten Windows*, again: "Poems, if they are any good at all, hold a knowledge elusive and multiple, unsayable in any other form." Yes. *Unsayable in any other form.*

It was not until I read and re-read this Rilke poem many times that it showed me how necessary confusion is. Unless you wish to confine it to the narrow orbit of what is generally known or already proven, *perplexity* is *necessary*. Indeed, it is integral to the complex intellectual and sensual processes that curiosity arouses. Uncertainty *liberates* as it beckons you toward the never-fully-known. Or knowable.

Mystic poets across time have unharnessed themselves from linear, predictable thinking to embrace the expansive wonder of not-knowing and never fully knowing. It was the 14th-century Sufi poet Hafiz who wrote, "I am happy before I have a reason." It is no surprise to learn also that it was 13th-century Sufi poet Rumi who counseled, "Sell your cleverness and buy bewilderment." As wonderfully, "Mysteries are not to be solved. The eye goes blind when it only wants to see why."

Often—most often—it is confusion that pushes you to take what the American poet Robert Frost celebrated as "the road less traveled." To know that you must live into your questions. *"Perhaps you will then gradually, without noticing it, live along some distant day into the answer."*

Curiosity, confusion, patience: all these under-sung human qualities take us into the mysteries of existence, without necessarily leading us out of them. Don't get me wrong! As much as anyone, I long for predictability and more reasonableness to hold onto in life. *Why does this fine person have so much to bear? Why is a selfless loved one's life cut short when some who harm others recklessly appear to thrive? Why is virtue not necessarily "rewarded"?* Many of our inner questions cannot be answered by logic or fairness. Nor by questions reduced to banalities or triteness. "The eye goes blind when it only wants to see why": Rumi's calls to exuberant living sing freshly and passionately around our shared earth. Yet few live by them. Instead, a deadening kind of certainty too often flourishes—though not in the minds of poets and mystics. Or those, like you, who read them with care.

*

It was as a young man, though already very much a poet, that Rilke wrote the prayer-poems known as *The Book of Hours*. Early in that remarkable collection he wrote the striking words that shape this conversation. Hear them again:

> I live my life in widening rings
> that spread out to encompass all things.
> I may not bring the last to completion,
> but that will be my attempt.
>
> I'm circling around God, around the ancient tower,
> and I've been circling for thousands of years,
> and I don't yet know: am I a falcon, a storm,
> or a vast song?

The quality of patience I am seeking is strong here. From a young man in a hurry to prove his worth as a poet, it is especially touching.

Rilke's image of "circling for thousands of years," without yet knowing who he was, speaks to me about life as well as about writing—and reading. When our reflections are nourishing, we circle and circle with interest, with curiosity, and sometimes with excitement. But a shadow emerges here, too. When we are stuck in obsessive or self-punishing ruminations, it's likely not "God" we circle—or any sense of an infinitely interrelated universe—but a debilitating sense of hopelessness that brings anguish and profound futility. To escape that takes a brave internal "standing back," a chosen surrender to not knowing *and* simultaneously to knowing the intrinsic value of every human life. Yours. Mine. Ours. Theirs.

And God, "that ancient tower"? With our greatest efforts to comprehend our place in the divine as well as human "scheme of things," there will be much circling. With luck, we may come to know a little more today than we knew yesterday. But not inevitably. Sometimes it is *not knowing* that opens us the greatest possibilities...even about who or what we most truly are.

The original German of this prayer-poem offers a special rhythm and rhyme in the first line: *Ich lebe mein Leben,* four short words in six syllables with a near doubling of the verb "live" and the noun "life." In English, too, this small poem sings as a testament to a big truth of existence: we are a mystery, even to ourselves; we are emerging, from the moment of conception throughout our life, then into and through death. As for completion, though, any sense of a finite circle closing may (wonderfully) be the most elusive of all. Rilke speaks of this for us. He calls us not to turn away from hope, not to withdraw or give up...but to embrace "all things"—"beauty and terror," as he elsewhere puts it—in the pursuit of expansiveness.

We can sense windows in the mind thrown open, creating portals to a bigger vision of the world, a larger and more inclusive vision of our own individual selves. It is not to mock our insufficiencies that the young poet, Rilke, dared us with his lines. It is, I am trusting, to stand alongside us, at the heart of our unknowing. *Your attempts have value. You have value. You and you and you.*

*

Writing about this same poem years ago, I suggested that at first it seems to be uncertainty's special hymn. *Circling...and circling...and I don't yet know...am I...?* But now I feel it more as an opening to wonder, to the

movements intrinsic in life, lessening that awful fear that any single ago-
nizing moment could hold us forever in its grip.

Wonder lets the world *in* and thereby deepens us. It makes room
for awe. *I live my life in widening rings / that spread out to encompass
all things.* There's such spaciousness here. And wholeness. The orbits of
your consciousness and mine will widen, the poem promises. Only if
we surrender—at least sometimes—to not knowing "everything," even
as we are prepared to *encompass all things.* This is a conscious refusal to
be pinned down that may resonate particularly strongly for those who
remain faithful to seeking even when, for them, the familiar props of
conventional faith cannot be leaned upon.

The central prop of ancient theisms is that "ancient tower." I, too,
have circled this for most of my conscious life. This poem allows me to
see that circling *is* my life. It is with the "ancient tower" as my constant
that I *can* "...spread out to encompass all things, all states of mind and
being. Of heart and soul.

For this commitment to continue circling, tenacity as well as patience
are required. Self-inquiry takes courage, even in the company of Rilke.
Take heart, though. While thinking for yourself can feel lonely, it is also
essential for those widening circles. It is essential for growing into all that
you are...becoming. A chrysalis can seem a far cosier place to be than the
wider world where a butterfly must live in vulnerable beauty and end its
days in death. There is an allure to other people deciding for you and
telling you that their views are *right.* Like the butterfly, we too are both
fragile and courageous. We can be timid and yet learn to become tena-
cious. In all our circling, we can temper boldness with tenderness.

> I'm circling around God...
> ...and I don't yet know: am I a falcon, a storm,
> or a vast song...

In Rilke's first version of this poem, he seemed to underline this by end-
ing it not with a question mark but with ellipses, signaling the ongoing
nature of his unknowing. Which summoned his own curiosity.

In speaking of this poem, Robert Bly chose to see Rilke as that "vast song." For the rest of us, we come back to ourselves and this present moment. Who is it circling the "ancient tower"? Who is it circling God, and "*circling for thousands of years*"? It is you. It is me. It is the people we know and love; it is also the people we don't know and those we might find it difficult or even impossible to love. But in every case, at the heart of the matter it is the one who is still becoming, who "doesn't yet know" what or who they are in this expansive journey.

*

Sydney is a global city always in an unsettling rush. A day before writing these words I crossed the city in an Uber. Sitting in the back of a stranger's car, neither of us chatting, I was free to consider those images: *falcon, storm, vast song*. Rilke would have chosen his words with care. Curiosity draws us closer to the mind of the poet. A *falcon*, riding high and powerfully in the sky, tempting the heavens with its nearness; a *storm*, gathering, unpredictable, uncontainable, carrying all with it; a *vast song*, giving voice to that yearning, seeking, circling, that unknowing devotion to the immense tower. To the All?

Which am I? Which are you?

Confusion adds richness to our curiosity here. For perhaps the nearest truth is that we are all that Rilke summons—and more. So very much more. The song pauses. Then continues.

CHAPTER 14

RISKING CREATIVITY

Though the world changes as swiftly
as cloud-forms,
all that's perfected returns
home to the most ancient of things.

Beyond the change and passing,
farther and freer,
your primal song endures,
god with the lyre.

Suffering has not been understood,
nor has love been learned,
and what distances us in death

is not unveiled.
Only the song, over the land,
hallows and celebrates.

—The Sonnets to Orpheus I.19

[*MARK S. BURROWS*]

How would it be if you could simply create a captivating painting, com-
pose a memorable symphony, or write a perfect poem? Or just decide
to live creatively—as if there is any "just" in that? How would it feel to

wake up one day, any day, and say to yourself, *Now is the time to create something beautiful*, and do just that? Beautifully?

We know that this isn't the way things generally happen. If it were, we'd not be speaking of the creativity of art but simply of its production, which is something quite different. If there is such a thing as "easy art," the lack of effort would rob you of one of art's—and life's—prime experiences: the pathway of curiosity and imagination that leads you to create something new; the patient sense of wonder that opens you to seeing differently; the marvel of shaping something enduring within the drift of this passing life. *Creatio ex nihilo*, or "creating out of nothing," is what the ancients called it when describing the "activity" of creation. It is that unexpected. Seemingly impossible. And, yes, radical.

This points to the primal pattern of *all* making, the root of what we mean when we speak of *living a creative life*, of crafting, of shaping a new whole with familiar parts. It has to do with bringing beauty out of chaos, form from formlessness, order out of confusion. If so, the ancient Hebrew notion that every human being is made "in God's image" might have everything to do with creativity. With "making," for which the Greeks use the simple word "*poiein*" from which we derive "poet," meaning to create. To "poetize," as it were, which is not magic but miracle.

A child's first efforts, which happen well before they can use their hands effectively, is the making of language. They play with sounds, delighting in rhyme and succumbing to the lure of rhythm, beyond any evident sense we can make of their earliest utterances. As they acquire a level of physical dexterity, they begin "making" with what is at hand. They seem to know this instinctively. As parents or caregivers, we surround them with engaging toys, inviting them into the alluring realm of games.

Yet at their core they have the capacity to "make" their world through playing with whatever is within reach. My children, when they were very young, like other children around the world, delighted in taking simple things that were available as the objects of their play. A wooden spoon and the metal top of one of our cooking pots became instruments on which they drummed away with joyful abandon. No one would have described the sounds they made as melodious, but it was a music of sorts that had rhythm and expressed their delight. Though loud, it was creative—and for that reason alone beautiful.

Many of us began to unlearn this uninhibited, intuitive spontaneity as we grew older. Under pressure to conform, we forgot what it is to play, often presuming it to be a needless distraction even to the point of dismissing it as an unjustifiable indulgence. We lost the capacity of imagining how we might make one thing out of something else: to see a snake in a stick; to be a prince one day and a rescuing heroine the next. We began to think that creativity was something far from our reach.

As we grew older, we tended to neglect our identity as *homo ludens*, as humans who *play*. The American naturalist Rachel Carson reminded us in *The Sense of Wonder* that "A child's world is fresh and new and beautiful, full of wonder and excitement. It is our misfortune that for most of us that clear-eyed vision, that true instinct for what is beautiful and awe-inspiring, was dimmed and even lost before we reached adulthood." Already as children we learned to "paint between the lines" in coloring books we've been given, with the figures and scenes neatly outlined, rather than starting with our own imagination and trusting that it was enough—indeed, more than enough. We found ourselves scolded for daydreaming in class and told to "stay on task." We renounced our wilder tendencies so that we could keep things in order. We even began to suspect that dreamers were underachievers.

We may have had parents who favored tidiness over the messiness of working with whatever is at hand—mud or clay, paint or water, blocks or fabrics, scattered pieces of paper or pens strewn across the living room floor. These days, parents, carers, and even teachers might well prefer the safety and efficiency of exploring the world through a computer screen rather than taking chances on venturing forth in the physical world, with all its unpredictability and variety—and wonder. The 19th-century Portuguese poet Fernando Pessoa points to the significance of this risk:

> From my village I see as much of the universe as can be seen
>   from the earth,
> And so my village is as large as any town,

> For I am the size of what I see
> And not the size of my height...

As he went on to remind us, "our only wealth is our seeing."

With so much constraining us "for our own good," we may become increasingly reluctant to express the wildness we may feel surging in our hearts. We might turn from these urges for fear of standing out and being ridiculed by others. When the risks seem to us simply too high, we may adjust our impulses to fit in with the crowd. Creativity, under the weight of such pressures, is the first casualty; delight is the second. Imagination cannot survive such barren pressures.

But in some part of us, surely, that wildness is not entirely forgotten. Nor is the freedom and unbridled exuberance we felt as children at play. We can never fully "unlearn" the desire to live creatively, which has to do with expressing our deepest feelings; experiencing the pleasure of "making" things; sharing our discoveries with others; and advancing our curiosity.

*

Some years ago, the prominent psychologist Mihaly Csikszentmihalyi wrote a bestseller on the experience of "flow," followed by a second on "finding flow" in your life. He pointed to this experience of engagement as one of the basic keys to happiness, describing it as depending upon what he called "optimal experiences." Athletes speak of this as "being in the zone," and jazz musicians as "finding the groove." All echo that ancient image of creating "out of nothing," opening to our aliveness through the instinctive sense of wonder which is our birthright.

What happens when *you* taste that wonder? When you find yourself carried in the "flow" of life with all its abundances? When you risk birthing beauty in your life—perhaps to the point that you begin to sense that life itself, in its plenty as in its poverty, is *beautiful*? Indeed, that *you* are beautiful?

This realization can come in all sorts of ways, some of which we call "art." At its core artfulness has to do with *living* creatively, living *connectedly*, which is what happens in those moments when you find yourself acting out of generosity rather than selfishness. When you discover yourself creating out of your imagination and not from a sense of duty. When you realize that you can face the cruelties of this world and the disappointments of your own life by choosing effort or sacrifice on behalf of others' needs rather than profit for yourself. When you decide to live by love rather than fear, compassion rather than greed. When you create life in that "dark interval" we discover in the face of suffering and death.

To act like this, to live from your creative instincts, is to refuse the cold logic of "the market," which is all about competing to win—however ruthlessly—and assuming some are more entitled to plenty and success than others. For to follow a creative path, *your* path, is to answer the twin calls of beauty and engagement, of discovery and community. It is to find the hidden link between compassion and delight.

*

Rilke himself was highly attuned to beauty's call. For him, it was essential nourishment. He wrote these lines in an essay he entitled "On Childhood and Education":

> Most people do not know at all how beautiful the world is and how much magnificence is revealed in the tiniest things, in some flower, in a stone, in tree bark, or in a birch leaf. There really is no more beautiful way of putting one's own life force to the test than by recognizing and seizing joy itself, without exaggeration but purely with the strength of joy, and to grasp with its proper measure the perfection and loveliness of a few days without even the least sense of a "too much."

How I used to marvel at watching my daughters, when they were quite young, "seizing joy itself," singing aloud as they went about the work of creating worlds in their imagination. How I delighted in observing the myriad ways this took shape in their hands as they brought splashes of colorful paint to paper, in the free movement of dance, in the expressive play of song. Witnessing their joy lifted my own spirits. In a poem dedicated to them entitled "Cloudwatch," included in my collection, *The Chance of Home*, I recall their delight—and mine—in watching billowy summer-clouds shape-shift as they drifted across the wide skies, describing their playful way of seeing "glimpses of enduring things that gather / us in the radiance of this passing world."

Creativity with all its playfulness lies at the heart of this beauty-birthing life. It happens in the moment and is often utterly spontaneous and unplanned. It reflects the truth that your life is not something you made—or make—on your own, that it is a gift that you received—and must receive again and again as you grow older. To be creative is to affirm with the poet Wendell Berry—against a narrower logic—that "the world is a holy vision, had we clarity to see it...." It is to believe, with Rilke, that your life is always carried by an unheard music, and that finally "only the song, over the land, / hallows and celebrates."

This sonnet, dedicated to Orpheus, that mythical son of Apollo, can be read, of course. But at its heart it is song, and invites us not simply to read but to *sing*:

> Though the world changes as swiftly
> as cloud-forms,
> all that's perfected returns
> home to the most ancient of things.

To live for this song, to enter its spacious and generative rhythm, is to defy the hurtful and even lethal separations between people that we've become conditioned to accept as "the way it is." It is to risk saying "Yes" to beauty. "Yes" to creativity. "Yes" to the imagination. "Yes" to love. That "Yes" comes to us in the moment when we open ourselves to "seize joy itself," when we catch a glimpse of how "... all that's perfected returns / home to the most ancient of things."

*

What's "more ancient" could be regarded as our primal need to create in our own lives, to see how our life is part of an eternal flow, and yet woven into specific communities that find their anchor in the past and reach into the future. To sense that, "beyond the change and passage, / farther and freer," a primal song drifts "over the land," singing itself *within* us regardless of our intentions.

This is the deep song that desires to flow *through* us, offering us the agency to create meaning. To exercise good will. To see our lives as part of "the Whole." And, yes, to *choose* to live in the abundance that is our birthright. It is to get in touch with that "primal song" (or *Vor-Gesang*, in Rilke's inventive lexicon) that is singing before we ever existed and will go on singing after our death. This is the song that welcomes us to participate, to create in the flow of creativity that precedes and follows us.

What is that "song" that is "over the land," as Rilke describes it? What is it that is always singing its way in this world—often enough as an "unheard music" that sings on, even when we cannot—in the first moment—hear it? What Rilke is gesturing toward is something he imagines as a song that precedes all else—in this case, Orpheus' original or "primal" song, preceding and somehow establishing all others. It is this song that *sings the world*—and invites us to *sing our life* as part of it all—again, and again, and again. Attending to the flow of this song, allowing it to kindle your imagination, is what lies at the heart of your own creativity.

Creativity, of course, depends upon the imagination. Einstein once observed, "when I examine myself and my methods of thought, I come close to the conclusion that the gift of imagination has meant more to me than any talent for absorbing absolute knowledge." The imagination is the source and means of creativity. But it is also neutral. In its bright forms, it delights and enhances life; in its darker shades, it can lead to horrific acts of violence. Or just everyday catastrophizing. In its richness, though, the imagination connects us to others, to communities of support as well as to outward gestures of compassion. It grounds us in the reality of our own life within the larger wholeness of creation. It connects, bridges, and heals. It rescues us from monotonous repetition and opens us to care for the vulnerability we experience in our own life as well as in the lives of others.

Such imagination, quickened with empathy, saves us from what the philosopher Martin Buber called "thingification," that tendency to reify—or objectify—everything, including our own life and that of others. Imagination is one of the powers that seeks another way. It is a potential we all carry within our hearts at all times. It is the "primal song" that invites us to "hallow and celebrate"—*our own life*.

"Let everything happen to you," Rilke elsewhere urges, both "beauty and terror." And by that he sensed how hard it might be to embrace that *Yes* in the face of suffering. And how important it is to do so precisely in such circumstances. Even when it sometimes feels too far away to summon. Even when that *Yes* rises in your throat but cannot yet find an outward form. Patience, too, is needed, for

> ...beyond the change and passing,
> farther and freer,
> your primal song endures,
> god with the lyre.

In a world heavy with variations on the dreary, stultifying theme of *No*, imagination is the originating pulse of *Yes*. Creativity is its hallmark, guiding us on the pathway into the flow of abundance. In the marketplace of things, of course, it has no value; it is not a commodity for sale. What it is, though, is a gift that multiplies itself in being given and shared. It is worth *everything*. And it gives us all that we need.

*

The difficulty we all face is that we too often sell our imagination short. We reason that we are not creative *enough*. This happens in many ways, one of which is the diminishing logic of comparison. Perhaps you felt this in school as a child: that relentless pressure to be better than others, or the distress you felt in not measuring up to others' achievements. Feeling your work compared, unfavorably, with others' work. Sensing that you are not able to meet some external standard or other.

You know how this works: you find yourself set on a scale by others—a parent, a teacher, a coach—or you set *yourself* on that scale with others whose accomplishments overshadow yours, and you eventually come to believe that their experience is more precious than yours. That they are more gifted than you. That your life is less significant than theirs. And, ultimately, that *you* are somehow deficient; that your life itself has less value.

Perhaps you assume it is "others" who are extraordinary. By some measures, that may well be the case. But you go further in presuming that they are somehow *different* from you. And then you begin to give yourself to the downward spiral of "if only" scenarios: *if only* I had the talents of a van Gogh, or the genius of a Mozart. *If only* I could dance like Martha Graham. *If only* I had the voice of Aretha Franklin. *If only...* It might more simply be this: "If only I could for once be praised and noticed."

*

Comparing ourselves to the magnificently talented—or to those who are routinely praised—is understandable. But this falls prey to the lie at the heart of such comparisons: that your efforts have no value, and, finally, that *you* are insignificant. Not gifted. *"Why even bother trying when someone else can do it better?"*

The word *amateur* is a precious reminder of another path. At its root, it denotes something undertaken for love, a word borrowed from the French—taken from the Latin root *amare*, meaning "to love." It signifies one who does not work for profit or even for praise. There is much freedom in that, in *not* striving for anything but the delight of the experience—of "seizing joy itself." Watch a small child allowed to play freely in the sand on a beach, or in newly fallen snow. Watch them building a dam in a shallow creek, or running faster than the wind, at least in their own sense of things. Thought falls away. *Being* arises. *Delight* surprises. *Joy* happens.

Comparing ourselves to the "greats" also ignores the struggle every committed artist faces in giving themselves to their work, particularly when it is not well received. In letters to his brother written late in his life, the Dutch artist Vincent van Gogh lamented that his paintings found no buyers. Yet he trusted his gift. He knew, as he put it, that "the day will come…when people will see they are worth more than the price of the paint and my living expenses, very meagre on the whole, which we put into them"—an understatement if ever there was one!

Of course, had you known any of the artists we now consider as great, you'd realize that they like most others faced harrowing doubts and often debilitating struggles. Mozart was widely heralded as a child genius. Even so, an established composer of an older generation dismissed his music as burdened with "too many notes," and he died in his 30s in poverty. Rilke, too, faced critics in his day, and continues to do so in ours, among those who found—or find—his poems too obscure or difficult. He wrote, though, not to please others but to be true to the creative impulses that gave shape to his art. He sought above all to be faithful to the source of creativity, to the "song" he sensed—and sometimes heard—flowing within him, that "hallows and celebrates."

*

In your life, far from a writer's desk, perhaps, or a painter's easel, it can be challenging to remain stubbornly creative and fresh in your noticing and appreciating. It may help to think of this not so much as a *doing* but as a way of *being*, an attentiveness to a hidden, inner source of creativity that brings craft, thoughtfulness, initiative alive in the most mundane tasks. One that transforms them—and *you* yourself—in "flow" experiences. One quickened by imaginative passion. One that lifts you, even amid the shadows, into something like radiance.

These come in all sorts of ways: as you undertake routine tasks at home or at work that most absorb you or where you must rise to an unfamiliar challenge. Or when you seek a new way of doing something either because the technology or the demands have changed. Perhaps someone in your life has needs that require you to think far "outside the box." Creativity may also be needed to resolve a struggle with another person without risking further hurt.

In the sacred rituals of daily life creativity is needed as you plan a garden-bed, planting seeds that you hope will flourish. Or as you re-arrange your house or set the table for a meal you've prepared, imagining the simple satisfaction your creative work will bring. Or as you take twice the time you need to finish a routine chore with particular care. Even devotion.

> Though the world changes as swiftly
> as cloud-forms,
> ...your primal song endures,
> god with the lyre.

What determines this creative flow that we could compare to an energy *for* life, not just a duty *of* life? Why is it that creativity seems to have more to do with what we *cannot* control, and often happens in the wilderness? In what might seem to be the wilderness of your life? And yes, in your *wildness*? That it has little to do with conforming to others' expectations, at least when these diminish you? For creativity generally arises not from what we "organize" with the large frontal lobe of our cerebrum, but with what finds its shaping energies within that vast and largely hidden realm belonging to the "deep" mind. To the "unconscious" mind, which Jung once suggested "sees correctly even when conscious reason is blind and impotent." Here, in the darkness of wilderness, is where creativity waits to be found—and *to find you.*

This wilderness is where Rilke's Vor-Gesang, Orpheus' "song before all other songs," comes into play. You'll come to know it when you set aside the map you imagined might have charted your life's journey and listen instead for the flow you won't find through linear thinking, logical reasoning, or "time management." You won't necessarily discover it, either, by finding your way to the right course at the right time. This song is sometimes messy, and often uncomfortable. Even dangerous. And it usually breaks through those neat boundaries we rely upon to hold our lives together.

It often belongs to what Rilke called the "dark hours" of our lives, those realms we cannot manage, which yet somehow "deepen [our] senses," as he elsewhere puts it. Even there, that "primal song endures, / god with the lyre." This has often been the case in my life as a poet, usually with a mix of anguish and delight. Yes, poems sometimes come from ecstatic experiences like falling in love, rising with the exuberant rush of spring and dancing through the long summer all the way to the joyful harvests of the fall. But others have a different origin.

They're the ones that come after the bright seasons have had their say, yielding to the solitude that comes upon us in the depths of winter with its brittle cold and long nights. These are the ones that face the burden of loss with all its anguish—those difficult "hours" you'd probably not choose if you had a choice.

> ...Beyond the change and passing,
> farther and freer,
> your primal song endures,
> god with the lyre.

What a claim this is! The opening stanza points to "all that is completed," all that seems finished and returning to its deeper source within this passing life. All that returns to the wellspring of creativity, through imagination's freeing flow. But what is it that initiates this return? For Rilke, this reflects Orpheus' primal song, the work of the "singing god" with his lyre whose melodious playing wooed the animals out of the forest. But this figure of ancient Greek mythology also knew to return to this song in his own time of desperation and grief, as when he lost his beloved Eurydice to death—because of his own doubt.

Orpheus came to represent, for Rilke, the fullness of art in its elemental truth: as a force that holds us through all we must face of suffering and loss. But song for him was no cheap fix for life's problems. According to one version of this legend, Orpheus ultimately failed at his hope to restore Eurydice to life because, in the very last moment, he faltered and turned to see if she was still following him, thereby losing her forever. Creative work requires not only risk, but trust—as Orpheus bitterly discovered. And, yes, it often ends not with success but with defeat. The hope is as alluring as the risk is great.

Rilke's sonnet is at once an ode to the creative power of the arts and, at the same time, a gift in its own right. It is a celebration of the power of creativity in our lives—as well as a reminder that we often face this with fear or ignorance or both:

> Suffering has not been understood,
> nor has love been learned...

The poet's point is not to chastise us or belittle us for our weakness. The poem ends as a testimony to what art *is* and remains, even when art fails us—or when we fail *art*. It is a witness to what we might still discover amid our suffering. And learn of love within the veil of this life.

This poem calls to each reader individually, a bold invitation that you risk opening yourself to the song that carries you. That you listen for the unheard music that is always present, drifting "over the land." For even when you don't know to trust it, or refuse to risk opening yourself to its gifts, the song continues to stir in and through and beyond you. To tune in to the song, to make it your own, may take some resistance to the common assumption that every potentially empty moment should be filled with other people's "creativity," however contrived or banal. From mid-century on, we in the West have been ever more susceptible to being "entertained"—the German word for this, *Unterhaltung*, suggests a posture of being subordinated or "held under"—rather than taking up crafts or arts alone or collectively, where we join with others to create, however imperfectly.

This seriously influences how we engage with and give ourselves to daily tasks where we are not expert. It subdues even in children a willingness to try something different for the sheer joy of the experience. In fact, it makes life itself something to be *consumed* rather than fully, even extravagantly, lived.

*

The *Sonnets'* inspiration came unexpectedly after Rilke learned that his daughter's friend, Vera Ouckama Knoop, had died of leukemia, the same illness that would take Rilke's own life less than five years later, in 1926. Vera had been a dancer, already celebrated in her youth, who in the face of the debilitating illness that gradually immobilized her turned to drawing, painting, and writing until her death at the age of nineteen. The courageous beauty of her life made a deep impression on Rilke, both because of the power of her creativity and because of her courage to risk living creatively in the presence of the losses she suffered and the premature death she faced.

Rilke remarked in letters to friends that the poems that became *The Sonnets to Orpheus* came to him like a sudden downpour after a long drought. But that drought is what gave shape and energy to these remarkable poems, and the long darkness through which Rilke had lived after the First World War—we would call it depression today—became the creative ground out of which these poems burst forth.

What does creativity have to do with the gift of our mortality? And why does art often bloom, unexpectedly and unaccountably, in the wildernesses we face in our lives? I can't say. But I know that the call of creativity often comes amid adversity and rises against the grain of conformity. It refuses the cheap lure of "normalcy." It calls us to risk *life* in the shadow of death, inviting us to create in the face of suffering and loss. It imagines light arising in the darkest season. It whispers to us to seek beauty amid the horrors we and others face.

The inner creativity that we carry deep within us must often wait, as with Rilke's life, through a long drought. It must often endure stubborn, dry seasons, perhaps even years and decades, until the moment of

decision and courage comes. What is that moment? What is its origi-
nating force? It might be some particular "thing," and that could be *any-*
thing. Perhaps something overheard or remembered—a phrase someone
once uttered, or a metaphor that seemed to find its shape *ex nihilo*, "out
of nothing." It could come from an experience of being in nature, in a
sustained moment of attentiveness. Poems sometimes begin this way,
which is not magic or even craft but miracle.

If you're like me, creativity often comes in times of solitude, which
Rilke spoke of as *Einsamkeit*, as when we take time to pause in our hurry
and give our attention fully to something singular and particular. It
might be as simple as glimpsing a single, reluctant leaf dancing on an
otherwise barren branch in an early-winter wind. It might be as ordinary
as noticing a tree's roots reaching down over a steep granite ledge to find
a "hold" in the ground below. It could be as particular as sensing the
rhythm of your own breath as it beats in tune with the endless rhythm
of the ocean's waves—to the point that the lines of a song begin to form
in your mind. It could be as singular as the exuberance with which your
dog bounds through the woods on an early morning walk. Such ordi-
nary moments, with all their "here-and-now-ness," matter.

Because ultimately creativity is *within* us all. And its possibility lies
within *everything*. Even those "shadowed" things you face. You might dis-
cover it simply as an intensification of your life. You might sense it in
moments when you feel your life carried in the "flow" of a larger creativity.
It rises from those moments of risking attentiveness amid long periods
of suffering or distress. Perhaps when you begin to glimpse a radiance
in things you'd never noticed before or recall the tide of long-forgotten
memories moving in the depths of your heart.

Whatever its origin, it takes practice to be ready for a burst of cre-
ative inspiration, for it might come *anytime*, as *anything*. To be open to
this is to pay heed to your poet's mind. And often enough this comes
unexpectedly, as something unimagined, perhaps even unhoped for. But
its coming is never undesired, especially when you've lost your way in
those "dark hours" and find yourself tempted to fall back on someone
else's path through the wilderness. Paying attention to what *is*—to who

you are—in such times is to make of your own life something sacred. To open yourself so that you are ready to "hallow" and "celebrate" it.

It is also a risk. What I've begun to realize over time, though, is that *paying attention to where I am* is more important for me than trying to figure out *who I am* or *what I should do*. This is what matters most— not only for creating, but also, and more importantly, for *living creatively*. Rilke knew this. His poems were his way of pointing to experiences— not his alone, but those that reveal to us what he calls "the Open," a way of living spaciously and receptively in our lives.

Rilke writes out of this conviction, trusting that poetry—or, perhaps more accurately, a poet's non-linear, non-conformist way of seeing—could become our doorway into a certain spaciousness *in our own lives*. He reminds us of the abundance that exists within us, even when nothing concrete is produced. Of course, attentiveness of itself does not produce art. At least not in some mechanical manner. But nothing meaningful and enduring comes into being without it. For the attention works within us by opening us to life's flow, in and through us and all the things of this earth.

It is also Rilke who helps us see that when creativity takes shape, somehow, through the ways we inhabit our lives, we begin to glimpse something that was already and always *here*. Call it a heightened awareness. Call it a playful sense that deepens our *knowing* of the real. Call it the sense of wonder. Whatever name you decide upon, the act of risking attention to what *is* becomes the source of your creativity, which is what matters most—for *you*. It is to know the experience of giving yourself over, in some particular place or experience, to a more spacious and seemingly timeless awareness. It is to sense the "song" that is carrying your life with a power that exceeds words, and to see that this, alone, "hallows and celebrates." In fact, the song is not yours to sing, at least not in the first instance. It sings *you*.

CHAPTER 15

YOU ARE THE FUTURE

You are the future, the vast dawning
above the plains of eternity.
You are the rooster's crow after the hours of night,
the dew, morning Mass, and the young girl,
the strange man, the mother, and death.

You are the shifting shape
rising forth ever alone from fate
to remain uncelebrated and unlamented,
and as indescribable as a wild forest.

You are the deepest essence within things
that withholds the final word of its being
and shows itself always differently to others:
to the ship you are land, to the land a ship.

—from "The Book of Pilgrimage," *The Book of Hours*

[*STEPHANIE DOWRICK*]

What does the phrase "a writer's life" mean to you? Do you imagine that
the generic writer most likely lives in and through their imagination and
reflections, rather than in—if not up to their necks in—the messiness,
contradictions, and unpredictability of so-called ordinary life?

In Rilke's life and work there is evidence of a consistent pull toward setting himself apart, but even so he spun his metaphysics from a web that grew from intensely sensual grounded-ness. Who is to say where "earth" ends, and "heaven" begins? Or where spirit is animating the physical form we call body? Or that same "body"—our physical form—both clothes and expresses spirit?

During this rich time of writing, we welcomed the birth of a baby girl into our immediate family. When I held her in my arms, or watched her in her devoted parents' arms, I could not fail to observe how naturally she gives and receives love. Her original nature *is* love. She is without self-consciousness—and with parents as loving as my son and his wife, together with our close-knit extended families, it may be years before she begins to ask the soul-searching, soul-shaking question, "Am I enough?" Enough for now? Enough for the future? Enough to bear the uncertainty intrinsic to life?

Rilke opens this phenomenal (and beloved) poem with a statement that goes far beyond reassurance: "You are the future." *Du bist die Zukunft.* Here Rilke's ambiguous "You/you" is center stage. The "you" that is intrinsically personal and divine; intimate and awesome.

For each "you," the future is born and reborn with each new breath. But is this continuous emerging of enough-ness something that can be comprehended any way but subjectively, experientially? Poetically? I doubt it. Take the words slowly, in the manner of *lectio divina*, as if the poet wrote them just this morning. Prayer. And reassurance, both.

> You are the shifting shape
> rising forth ever alone from fate
> to remain uncelebrated and unlamented,
> and as indescribable as a wild forest.

In these lines "enough" falls away, becoming as irrelevant as it is to the unselfconscious, delighted child. The transactional world of commerce we live in thrives on, depends upon, a ruthless culture of insufficiency.

You can never have enough. You can never be enough. More, more, more is the constant Muzak to which capitalism dances. It would be a rare person who would ask, "Enough for what? For whom?"

That makes Rilke's unorthodox view as refreshing as an unscheduled downpour in the middle of the "dry." He well knew that "...our life is vast and can encompass every bit of the future that we can carry." As for literary critics—or critics of any other kind who would keep us small in vision and hope: "Read as little literary criticism as is possible. Such things are either partisan opinion that has grown petrified and meaningless, desiccated and emptied of life. Or else they are merely clever word-games in which one view wins today—and tomorrow the opposite view. *Works of art are of an infinite solitude.* No means of approach is as useless as criticism."

*

Enough is a word loaded with ambiguity. It churns up emotions that go further than language can. "Enough"—when we finally notice it—is quite wonderful. If we can allow that. Any respite from anxious wanting, needing, never mind grasping or fearing, is precious. Yet isn't "enough" frequently experienced in its *absence*, both in its embodied and existential forms?

> *Am I good enough?*
> *Am I worthy?*
> *Am I beautiful enough?*
> *Am I the kind of person who...?*
> *Do I have enough talent?*
> *Will others see my qualities...or only my shortcomings?*
> *Do I dare...? Have I got the strength to get through this?*

It is in the poignant crumbling of "enough" that Rilke typically writes, not to reassure but to celebrate and make vivid what so-called common "rationality" fervently denies.

You are the shifting shape
rising forth ever alone from fate
to remain uncelebrated and unlamented,
and as indescribable as a wild forest.

You are the deepest essence within things,
that withholds the final word of its being
and shows itself always differently to others:
to the ship you are land, to the land a ship.

Rilke's "you" is *you*. Perhaps. Or that "you" is God. Perhaps. Though never the God of dogma, leading to divisions and implying unforgiving judgment. "You" is or may be the One Poet who speaks through images and all true poets. Perhaps. "You" is the shapeshifter defying destiny and conformity alike. Perhaps. "You" may be life itself trembling—or exulting—in the eternal present. Perhaps. What "you" is not is a straight-jacket around "enough."

American literary critic and professor of comparative literature, Kathleen Komar, asks, "What is it about [Rilke's] poetry that so speaks to us in the post-modern era?" Her answer: "I would suggest...that at least one aspect of his appeal lies in his attempts to understand how human consciousness can survive its temporal prison and reach out to a metaphysical realm without abandoning this human, physical world."

When I wrote my first book on Rilke, it was that reaching into the metaphysical world that did more than inspire me. This is what our seeking is, without abandoning "this human, physical world" where we will discover our own "enough-ness." Such seeking pushed me forward *even when my fears and feelings of insufficiency* were harshest. What also made a difference, however, was the "real-time" companionship of my treasured academic supervisor for the original research who "held the lantern," "kept the faith," when I sometimes could not.

Companionship at this depth matters. Fidelity to self-respect and the care of others matters. Our own capacities to offer loyalty, inspiration, encouragement, support are most certainly to be cherished—and cultivated. Let us meet others' fears generously. Creatively. Wisely. Lovingly. That is our privilege as conscious beings. We will seldom face into and meet our deepest questioning of sufficiency, or our dreads of insufficiency, entirely alone. Even in times of faithful, contemplative solitude, we will likely draw upon the wellspring of riches we have received from others.

Our great hope as writers is that this book might be part of that for you, as the writing of it has been—and remains—for us. Our individual "enough" is abundantly peopled—if we welcome that. Giving to others what we long to receive may deplete us; it may also be healing. Poets play their part here. In an article in *Philosophy Now*, British philosopher Peter Rickman wrote that "poetry aims at the effective expression of what has not been expressed before or expressed inadequately. The reader of a good poem is apt to say: yes, that is what I thought or felt, but I could not express it, or express it adequately. The poet is a pioneer in the continuous creation of language *through which we catch reality*" [my italics].

*

Any defiance of what the world calls "reality" is vigorously discouraged and censored. It is also my observation, however, that entrenched experiences of "not enough" bring with them a mental and emotional agony that robs us of a steady or hopeful sense of self. One's inner reality becomes disrupted. It seems that the more fearful we are—and the more fragmented by exhaustion, disappointment, grief, shame, or anxiety— the more "out of touch" we will be with our own core and inner sanctum. This *directly affects how we reflect upon our deepest questions* because it disrupts our fundamental connectedness, expressed in this poem via a rich array of archetypes that belong to all and to no one.

> You are the shifting shape
> rising forth ever alone from fate
> to remain uncelebrated and unlamented,
> and as indescribable as a wild forest.

You are the deepest essence within things,
that withholds the final word of its being
and shows itself always differently to others:
to the ship you are land, to the land a ship.

The "shifting shape" of you which is "as indescribable as a wild forest": how brilliantly such a claim challenges cheap superficiality and single-dimensional platitudes. To be "out of touch" risks loneliness, a state far from solitude where you are alone with the essential reality of your own complex, evolving "self." Loneliness like this is pervasive, and ultimately perverse. It buckles the soul, makes it harder to feel that "I" can ever be enough for "myself" or for "you." Or that "you" could ever be enough for me. "No one understands," is a cry of despair that must be taken seriously.

*

Three stories meander through what follows, the first of them possibly apocryphal. It is told about a young man, born late in the 12th century who came eventually to be known as Francis of Assisi. Clearly a remarkable person in so many ways, Francis understood long before most people of his era (or ours) that he was not above but was connected to all of creation, to the greater whole. And not just to what can be perceived with the naked eye, either. He knew that the cosmos far outstretches our comprehension of it.

His ardent, protective love of nature and for all species was driven by an inner knowing that *life*, in its myriad expressions, had divinity within it. Like First Nations peoples around the world, Francis of Assisi viewed our human family's role on earth as custodians, not plunderers. Seen like that, all of life is sacred. Our caring of and for it becomes sacramental.

It is tempting to assume that such clarity of vision would have saved Francis from the large rumbling questions of "self": self-worth, self-respect, self-acceptance. It's easy to imagine that he burst fully formed into the Francis of cement birdbaths and holy pictures' fame: smiling gently as birds sit on his shoulders and flowers bloom year-round at his feet. But we would be kidding ourselves if we imagined that any serious person—including ourselves—does not have to face, at some time, these profound questions which transcend mere identity and go to the hidden depths not only of *Who am I?* but also *Am I enough?*

Spiritual beings on a human journey may be a concept almost too much to take. I understand that. Yet, from a transpersonal-psychological perspective, the questions *Who I am?* and *Am I enough?* must transcend the hard-won identity labels for which we sacrifice so much. Even the smallest shift in perspective lets us look freshly at what we most closely identify *with*: family place, profession, culture, race, gender, sexuality, social class, religion, political allegiance, or community involvement…as well as a less easily described, sometimes elusive, "sense of self."

This raises questions to be savored, *lived into*, shared with others. After all, some of our truest *Am I enough?* discoveries will not be made alone. They will be made through our intimacies with others. They will be lived out in the cradle of our relatedness. How generously are we seen? How generously do we see others? Where and when are we projecting our worst insufficiency-fears onto other people: reading *their* minds, not our own? How willing are we to make changes when we recognize that some old patterns keep us fearful or self-harming?

Living into these decisive questions, we may discover that we have become more used to seeing ourselves through other people's eyes rather than through our own. In fact, it is considerably more complicated than that. When we are feeling fragile or fragmented, we are likely to draw conclusions based on our *assumptions* which may be far bleaker than anything that is passing through someone else's mind. That speaks of a painful loss of self-compassion, and of a limited view of the complex, evolving, *whole self* each one of us is *becoming*, including you—with all your fears and doubts. Even the simplest lines from Rilke invite us to embrace a larger view—of a whole self as part of an unlimited whole.

His and similar inspiration might—and can—lead us toward a manner of self-inquiry and self-knowledge that is both truer and freer.

You are more than your sensations, thoughts, feelings, experiences—however compelling. What is that "more" for you? *Shedding familiar identity "labels," what's left? What is it that gives your individual life its specific as well as universal meaning? Is* Who am I? *changing with life passing? Are there some situations in which enough/not enough is predictably painful? And other situations where it is not?* These are not questions requiring answers. They are prompts, some of which may speak to you now—others, only years from now, if at all. They are lanterns to guide you as you live into your whole being.

Most of us will happily ignore the more profound inner questions as long as life conforms nicely to our agenda. Meaningful self-inquiry may have to wait until our confidence is shaken in some significant way. It may be that our trust in a benevolent universe or compassionate deity is turned upside down when circumstances beyond our control rob us of a relationship or good health, a home or country. We look in the mirror and are uncertain who it is we see.

> You are the shifting shape
> rising forth ever alone from fate
> to remain uncelebrated and unlamented,
> and as indescribable as a wild forest.

*

We often assume it is only the vulnerable or ill-prepared, the fragile or unwell, who will be haunted or tormented by such harrowing uncertainty. But even the remarkable young man Francis, surely calling from the depths of his heart and soul, was moved to look heavenwards to cry out, *My God and All; Who are you, Lord? And who am I?*

Who are you, God? you may echo. And truly, *who am I?* For these are the questions in every human heart that stays open to the immense gifts of self-inquiry. No authentically engaged person is exempt. The question—arguably the "deepest" of all—may not be God-directed, yet no less sincere for that. *What is meaning? What is life?* What is *my life…*

made (or not) in "the image of God," but certainly as a unique manifestation of life's force and wonder?

The second story I want to share is much more recent. For more than twenty years I led residential spiritual retreats in a particularly magnificent part of New Zealand, a region where hills, horizon, ocean, green and blue of every shade meet and connect. We gathered usually twice a year at a retreat center called Mana, the Māori word for spiritual power. Like the Francis tale, a deeply felt account becomes more universal and both more, and also less, personal in the re-telling.

Toward the end of a long day, several days into that retreat, one of our younger participants, a German science teacher and mother, asked a question that reflected through her self-denigrating wording her painful feelings of insufficiency. How courageous she was to do that. In fact, perhaps at this very time "enough" has come to seem like that illusory oasis that torments those crossing a merciless desert, parched for refreshment or survival. She had been to several of my retreats. I knew her to be as thoughtful as she is quietly accomplished. But we are not talking rational self-judgment here. Nor need we narrow our vision to include only those whom we believe "deserve" our validation, encouragement, or praise.

In one of those totally impromptu moments that bring teaching to life, I asked everyone present to stand in a large silent circle around our big octagon space, then—starting with her—I named each person in turn, taking my time, taking as much time as we all wanted, assuring each one, "*You are enough.*"

What made it so moving that many of us were soon weeping is that this simple, true statement, "*You are enough,*" brought up a recognition of the many conscious and unconscious ways we "water" the seeds, the torment, of our insufficiency. *Who am I?* Dare we imagine, even briefly, *I am enough? Who am I?* may be the biggest of the questions that any of us will ever live into. And it is everywhere here, leaning and leading us into a kinder, more self-respecting as well as a more compassionate way. It is obliquely, poetically addressed by Rilke in many of his poems, not least the last of his *Sonnets to Orpheus* (II.29) that concludes with the vivid lines,

> If what is earthly has forgotten you,
> say to the quiet earth: I flow.
> To the rushing waters speak: I am.

Now for the last of my three stories. This time it includes Lou Andreas-Salomé, who played such a pivotal part in Rilke's own "Who am I?" story. When they met, he was an insecure, emotionally damaged young man, only twenty-one years old though already set on devoting himself to a life of poetry. She was a married woman of thirty-six who had already published books on literary subjects and philosophy. Rilke was bedazzled by her—as were many other prominent men, including Nietzsche and later Freud.

Quite why she moved from initially regarding Rilke as someone she wished "would go completely away" to their becoming lovers, and when that fell apart confidants and committed friends for the rest of Rilke's lifetime, is not entirely clear. What is certain is that Lou liberated him, and, in important ways, he also liberated her. It was, nonetheless, Lou, who established the boundaries that Rilke could not.

Rilke more than admired Lou. He projected onto her a depth of wisdom that was unlikely to be realizable by any one human being. Sigmund Freud later said of Lou in relation to Rilke that "she was both the muse and the attentive mother of the great poet." Freud also said of her that she understood people better than they understood themselves—which is certainly what Rilke believed and craved, well beyond the time when their love affair, in its most immediate and dramatic form, had ended, all the way, with extreme poignancy, to the final weeks of his life.

In like measure, it is in the soul-nakedness of our most intimate relationships as lovers, partners, friends, parents, and adult children, that we come to greater clarity and insight about *Who I am* and *Who we are*, and what—and who—is *enough*. We come to this never fully or finally, but in glimpsing the reality of our "whole" selves, and in answering and welcoming the "wholeness" of another.

> You are the future, the vast dawning
> above the plains of eternity.

*

Lou was "enough" for Rilke in some core way—despite her adamant restrictions on his demands, despite his marriage to the remarkable artist Clara Westhoff who shared his single-minded commitment to "the work" while also becoming the mother of his only child, Ruth, and despite an adult lifetime of genuinely significant relationships with other gifted, generous women.

In middle-age, Lou had become a renowned psychoanalyst—when analysis was still itself more art than science, and when at least some degree of synthesis between the arts and medicine was welcomed. It is more than touching to know that Lou claimed to have cured some of her patients by reading Rilke's poetry to them, telling Rilke in one of her many letters to him, "They hear *your* tone as that of Life."

It is possible to amplify that thought, even while raising something of an eyebrow at the notion of reading any poetry as curative. I would suggest that what Lou conveyed to each of those fortunate people sitting in a quiet room with her was her own sense of appreciative wonder at the vision of life that emerges so "ripely" through what Rilke potentially gives every reader.

Lou's passion and qualities of warmth and presence would themselves have been supportively hypnotic. The specific miracle of Rilke's work, though, for me and for so many others, can be found on most pages as you absorb his words and "take them in." This comes, surely, from the simultaneous opening he brings to the unlimited depths and gifts of inwardness, or "innerness," together with a ravishing glimpse of worlds, more worlds, still more worlds, that his words convey.

The "Open" is both within and beyond. It could not be otherwise. We—you and I—are of Life, *and* able to contemplate it. This was the wisdom as well as the exhilarating illumination that Lou received from the mature poet Rilke became. Without directly sharing his metaphysical insights or impulses, but certainly comprehending and celebrating them, she celebrated too his inimitable sense of the Whole. In reflecting on his influence upon her, she wrote:

> Whoever reaches into a rosebush may seize a handful of flowers; but no matter how many one holds, *it's only a small portion of the Whole. Nevertheless, a handful is enough to experience the nature of the flowers* [my italics]. Only if we refuse to reach into the bush, because we can't possibly seize all the flowers at once, or if we spread out our handful of roses as if it were the whole of the bush itself—only then does it bloom apart from us, unknown to us, and we are left alone.

Every living form is part of the Whole. Comprehending its nature, *our nature*, is a gift of consciousness unique to our species, one that may well be unique to our planet. To paraphrase Lou, "A glimpse is enough to experience the nature of our being"—perhaps the nature of Life, certainly to locate ourselves on an "island of meaning."

Despite our longing to grasp onto life, to refuse the inevitability of death, or to divide ourselves from those unwelcome parts of it, or to find answers *now* to its devastating challenges and seemingly intractable problems, we must repeatedly learn to pause. To wait patiently, but with a curiosity lively enough that we can be startled. Lou's final warning is real: *let yourself risk reaching* without always knowing what you will find. Do not confuse a "handful" of experiences with your life as a whole, nor forget yourself as part of that Whole. Take a bigger view that is at once more vivid and vivifying.

*

What Rilke shows—as lavishly as any poet has ever done—is how our experiences are at once subjective, intimate, intense—deeply resonant in our bodies as well as our souls—yet universal. This does not imply sameness. On the contrary, our diversity is Life's greatest achievement. It may perhaps lead us toward a richer, more life-giving, and life-celebrating understanding of empathy, of meaning, of meaningful care.

As with so much of the commentary we have offered on Rilke, his work, its direct effect on our lives, this prescience about what our time needs and calls for is far more than *striking*. It brings us home to ourselves, to our own *continuing*, to our precious *becoming*. This is the placeless yet felt "place" where our deepest questions are found and faced, with a compassion and trust that likely can come only with conscious experiencing. And with the realization that, like every living form, we evolve: from the moment of conception to the leaving of this earth, we press forward into a future that is and simultaneously is not one we can create, yet inevitably and inarguably is one we share.

For the last word, we can return not to the poem that began this conversation, but again to the last of his sublime *Sonnets to Orpheus*, concluding as it does with the poignant lines

> And if the earthly has forgotten you,
> say to the quiet earth: I flow.
> To the rushing waters speak: I am. (II.29)

In the flow of this life, even when we might feel ourselves forgotten, *we are*—with all the questions we must learn to *live*, the perils we together face, and the joys and burdens we daily experience—part of the Whole. Whoever we are, wherever we are, we are carried inevitably by the flow of Life. This life. This now. This.

LIST OF POEMS CITED IN ORDER OF APPEARANCE

All translations of Rilke's poems—either in their entirety, as here noted, or in extracts—as well as all prose citations included in this book, are by Mark S. Burrows unless otherwise noted. Most of them come from one of the two collections of Rilke's poems that he has published. Those cited from the collection *Prayers of a Young Poet* (Paraclete Press, 2013; revised edition 2024) were later included—lightly edited—in "The Book of Monastic Life," which became Part I of *The Book of Hours*. The untitled sonnets are from Rilke's *Sonnets to Orpheus* (Monkfish Book Publishing Co., 2024).

Chapter 1: "God speaks to each of us before making us"; untitled, from "The Book of Monastic Life," Part I of *The Book of Hours* (in *Prayers of a Young Poet*); this translation adapted by Stephanie Dowrick

Chapter 2: "The hour bows down and serves me"; untitled, from "The Book of Monastic Life," Part I of *The Book of Hours* (in *Prayers of a Young Poet*)

Chapter 3: "Oh you who feel deeply"; untitled, *The Sonnet to Orpheus* I.4

Chapter 4: "Desire the change"; untitled, *The Sonnets to Orpheus* II.12

Chapter 5: "O the losses into the All"; untitled, written in a letter of 1925 to Marina Tsvetaeva; translated by Stephanie Dowrick

Chapter 6: "Archaic Torso of Apollo," *New Poems*

Chapter 7: "I believe in all that is not yet said"; untitled, from "The Book of Monastic Life," Part I of *The Book of Hours* (in *Prayers of a Young Poet*)

Chapter 8: "My life is not this steep hour"; untitled, from "The Book of Monastic Life," Part I of *The Book of Hours* (in *Prayers of a Young Poet*)

Chapter 9: "Entrance"; from *The Book of Images* I.1

Chapter 10: "Wait a moment....!"; untitled, *The Sonnets to Orpheus* I.15

Chapter 11: "I find you in all these things"; untitled, from "The Book of Monastic Life," Part I of *The Book of Hours* (in *Prayers of a Young Poet*)

Chapter 12: "You darkness that I come from"; untitled, from "The Book of Monastic Life," Part I of *The Book of Hours* (in *Prayers of a Young Poet*)

Chapter 13: "I live my life in widening rings"; untitled, from "The Book of Monastic Life," Part I of *The Book of Hours* (in *Prayers of a Young Poet*)

Chapter 14: "Though the world changes as swiftly"; untitled, *The Sonnets to Orpheus* I.19

Chapter 15: "You are the future"; untitled, from "The Book of Pilgrimage," Part II of *The Book of Hours*

ACKNOWLEDGMENTS

[*MARK S. BURROWS*]

Behind every creation, including that of books, lies an intricate genesis story. This one is no exception to that rule. Stephanie and I first met almost two decades ago, and over the years since then our countless discussions exploring Rilke's writings—among other things—blossomed into a valued friendship, an experience that has deepened my respect for her insights into Rilke's writings and for the generous sharing that has been ours in the "heart-work" we both treasure. I am profoundly grateful to her for shaping this writing partnership, one that stands in answer to the alluring question Rilke posed in one of his late poems: "Who sings the distant heart that lingers, whole, in the midst of all things?" Among fellow poets and Rilke scholars who have influenced my grasp of Rilke's writings, Gotthard Fermor merits special mention. During the last decade when I was teaching at a university in Bochum (Germany), Gotthard invited me to join the "Bonn Rilke Project," an artistic collaboration that led to the publication of a three-volume edition of Rilke's *Book of Hours* (*Das Stunden-Buch*). Gotthard's companionship in sharing this work with me and the insights into Rilke's writings that we have explored over the decades have deepened my grasp of the poet's peculiar genius. We join in thanking Pádraig Ó Tuama, Robert D. Romanyshyn, Sally Gillespie, and Barbara Mahany for their thoughtful encouragement as this book took shape, and I also thank our editor, Anne McGrath of Monkfish Book Publishing Company, for her early and abiding belief in this book. Finally, my journey of "living the questions" has always been shaped by my family: I am grateful to my now adult children, Emma and Joey, who have been a never-ending source of encouragement and inspiration, and to my spouse, Ute Molitor, who has shared my life and passions over the past quarter century, gracing me throughout with her generosity of heart and mind: "O Erfahrung, Fühlung, Freude—, riesig!"

[*STEPHANIE DOWRICK*]

As someone privileged to live alongside the world's longest surviving cultures, I acknowledge elders past and present of the Larrakia nation and the Gadigal people of the Eora nation on whose lands I live and work. With unlimited gratitude, I acknowledge my co-writer, Mark S. Burrows. Throughout the years of writing, it has been a bold, challenging project to "circle" Rilke with our own innermost questions and persistent prompts to one another. What an experience it has been, sometimes humbling, sometimes a vital refuge. This work builds on my earlier published writing on the poet, *In the Company of Rilke* (published in 2009 by Penguin Random House). My thanks to Mark for his friendship and trust are as great as my thanks (and admiration) for his gifts as a poet, scholar, and translator. I also wish to thank my very dear friend Professor Jane R. Goodall who has supported my Rilke work over more than two decades, without her enthusiasm flagging. Joyful thanks, too, to my writer friends, Lisa Alther, Joyce Kornblatt, and Dr. Sally Gillespie for their constancy and inspiration, and to Subhana Barzaghi Roshi who gave my work, and me, particular shelter at a needed time. My family— precious children Gabriel and Kezia, their partners Nakkiah and Tony, and beloved three grandchildren, Madeleine, Charlie and Lux—inspire me daily. The most loving thanks are not enough. I particularly wish to acknowledge the lifetime and life-saving support of my clever, kind sister, Geraldine Killalea. My husband, Dr. Paul Bauert, science- and medicine-trained, has revealed himself to be this writer's best reader. Better, he reminds me of a need for aliveness and absurdity even in the most serious times. What wisdom in that. "Unfolding" is a favorite Rilkean word. How marvelous to share an unfolding life with Paul. Thank you.

A NOTE ON THE AUTHORS

Mark S. Burrows MDiv, PhD, is an award-winning poet, translator, and theologian, acclaimed internationally for his studies of medieval mysticism as for his explorations of spirituality and the arts. Until 2020 he served as professor of religion and literature at the Protestant University of Applied Sciences in Bochum, Germany. He is also active as a workshop and retreat leader, in the US and internationally, and widely recognized for his work as a translator and interpreter of Rilke. In 2013 he published the first English version of poems Rilke originally called "The Prayers" (*Prayers of a Young Poet,* 3rd revised edition, 2024), and recently brought out a new translation of Rilke's *Sonnets to Orpheus* (2024). He also contributed introductions to three volumes of a new German edition of *Das Stunden-Buch* (2014–2018). Mark's translation projects also include an English edition of the celebrated Iranian-German poet SAID's 99 Psalms, and the first bilingual edition of poems by the Jewish-German poet Hilde Domin, *The Wandering Radiance: Selected Poems of Hilde Domin.* Together with Jon M. Sweeney, he has published three collections of meditative poems inspired by the medieval mystic Meister Eckhart, most recently *Meister Eckhart's Book of Darkness and Light* (Hampton Roads Publishing Co., 2023), which the Nautilus Book Awards cited as a Gold Winner in 2024. A member of the Iona Community, he lives and writes in Camden, ME. https://soul-in-sight.org

Stephanie Dowrick PhD, DMin, has won major US awards for three of her books, including two Nautilus Awards: *Choosing Happiness:*

Life & Soul Essentials, Creative Journal Writing, and *Heaven on Earth: Timeless Prayers of Wisdom & Love.* A former publisher, founder of The Women's Press in London, UK, she is trained as a psychotherapist and was ordained in 2005 as an Interfaith minister at New York's Cathedral of St. John the Divine. Stephanie's international publications also include *Intimacy & Solitude, Forgiveness and Other Acts of Love, Seeking the Sacred: Transforming Our View of Ourselves and One Another,* and the highly praised *In the Company of Rilke,* an exploration of Rilke and reading. Her most recent book (US edition, St Martin's Press, 2025) is *Your name is not Anxious: A very personal guide to putting anxiety in its place.* She has written fiction for adults and children, and her books have been translated into multiple languages. She contributes widely to mainstream and social media through print and broadcast media, is known for her public speaking and workshop retreat leadership, in person and via Zoom. Born in Aotearoa/New Zealand, Stephanie has lived in six different countries including sixteen years in Europe, mainly in the UK, also Germany. She now lives in Australia. http://stephaniedowrick.com

www.ingramcontent.com/pod-product-compliance
Lightning Source LLC
Jackson TN
JSHW020017141224
75386JS00025B/573